FIVE MYTHS
OF CONSUMER
BEHAVIOR

D0768374

FIVE MYTHS
OF CONSUMER
BEHAVIOR:
CREATE
TECHNOLOGY
PRODUCTS
CONSUMERS
WILL LOVE

PAUL ALLEN SMETHERS
ALASTAIR FRANCE

ConsumerEase Publishing | Seattle, Washington

FIVE MYTHS OF CONSUMER BEHAVIOR:

CREATE TECHNOLOGY PRODUCTS CONSUMERS WILL LOVE

PAUL ALLEN SMETHERS & ALASTAIR FRANCE

Copyright © 2007 by ConsumerEase Publishing

Published by:

ConsumerEase Publishing
Post Office Box 9906
Seattle, WA 98109-0906

All rights reserved. No part of this book may be reproduced in any form, except for the inclusion of brief quotations in a review, without permission in writing from the author or publisher.

The authors and publishers have taken care in the preparation of this book, but make no expressed or implied warranty of any kind and assume no responsibility for errors or omissions. No liability is assumed for incidental or consequential damages in connection with or arising out of the use of the information contained herein. This book incorporates all legal agreements under its draft title, *Rapid Consumer Adoption*.

ISBN-10: 0-9763578-2-8
ISBN-13: 978-0-9763578-2-7

Library of Congress Control Number: 2006900508

(PB)   10   9   8   7   6   5   4   3   2

For information about special quantity discounts please visit www.5myths.com

Table of Contents

Foreword

Since its launch in July 2002, my group has been responsible for consumer marketing of the *Vodafone live!* mobile Internet portal in Italy. During this period, the portal evolved from a niche product into a mass-market product with over 160 services and over 3 million customers. The main challenges we are faced with daily for such a complex consumer product are:

Needs and experience levels vary widely among users and are frequently nonoverlapping.

Users want consistency so they can easily return to their favorite services, but they also need variation and novelty in the offering based on time of day and special events.

Users may access a complex matrix of portal services that from a range of over 200 models of mobile handsets, and the best possible user experience must be provided on all these variations.

Thanks to the collaboration with Paul and Alastair, we have developed a deeper understanding of customer behavior for implementing design principles, portal structure, and services. This was achieved through usability testing and business intelligence analysis and by sharing best practices with other mobile operators around the world.

Undoubtedly, many factors come into play that determine service success, and many of these factors are outside our direct control. Still, the methodology for consumer adoption proposed here has definitely helped us drive service usage and market penetration for *Vodafone live!*

With the help of this book, you, too, can benefit from years of research and application in rapid consumer adoption.

Csaba Tarnai
Milan, Country Manager *Vodafone live!*

Author's note

It has taken me 25 years of working on products like PC and Macintosh software, Internet services, and mobile phones to uncover the myths revealed in this book. Early in my career, I steered several products to success and was promoted to roles such as vice president of marketing and business unit manager. In these early ventures, my primary contribution was in figuring out why consumers do or don't adopt our products and fixing the products to gain more success.

About 8 years ago, I started consulting for major technology companies as a consumer behavior expert, working in practically every country and often traveling over 200,000 miles a year. I developed an instinct for product success. Soon I met the coauthor of this book, Alastair France, and we spent 7 years together analyzing billions of transactions made by millions of users. With this data we were able to prove the fundamental principles that govern consumer behavior with technology products and services.

Alastair (who goes by "Ali"), has become my strongest and most trusted colleague in promoting and refining the methodologies we use in the field. He is a strong usability person, with his own bank of years focusing on turning technical ideas into consumer-grade products. I'm indebted to Ali for his additions to this text.

Ali and I hope you will benefit from the insights we share here and find success for your products and services.

Paul Allen Smethers

Preface

Most marketing and engineering professionals have been there—the product idea is complete, the first version is almost ready to ship, and the marketers are going crazy trying to decide how much marketing "noise" to make and fearing that the press or the users will not like the product. By the time the product ships, the funding usually is running low and an all-out attempt is made—as much noise as is affordable—in the hope that the hype will help ensure its success.

Shipping a new product or service is a *revolutionary* task. Many things have to come together to make that first offering work to deliver on the initial promise. The genesis of the product is a great idea that must be refined with thousands of decisions, most of which are new even to the decision makers. With that many unknowns, the designers can't help but become revolutionaries. Starting a new market with a new product requires faith, dedication, and a lot of guesswork.

Attracting a large base of consumers, on the other hand, is an *evolutionary* process. New products *spring* into existence all the time, most doomed to failure. Great products *evolve* into their success. The key success factors become detectable when the first consumers start using the first versions of the product, but the product designers never stop to observe or accept them. Designers find it hard to *stop* revolutionizing their product; they find it even harder to *start* evolving it.

Thus, the product fails to meet its initial goals. Soon the designers follow it up with a new version, with new features representing the next level of guesswork at what the consumer really needs. But success still eludes the designers; sales continue to be mediocre. The gap between a new product's design and the needs and expectations of its consumers grow awkwardly farther apart.

Consumers, on the other hand, have a very different view. Every day, thousands of new technologies are pitched to them over the Internet, on TV, or in magazines. Today's consumers have been conditioned to say "no" faster than ever before. They don't want more technology. They can barely manage the products they have already accepted into their lives. They use mobile phones, e-mail, Google, instant messaging, Internet shopping, and are grappling with even more technologies for entertainment, such as MP3, DVD, and high-definition TV. They see no reason to try harder to accept new products. Further, they don't understand why the technologies keep getting more complicated. They just want simpler, quicker value. Why is that so hard to deliver?

The gap between consumers and product designers (entrepreneurs, marketers, and engineers) has grown too far apart. If you are a designer of a new Internet service or other technological gadget—and you want your product to succeed—you should first understand how consumers behave when they approach and use your product.

This book helps reduce this gap by presenting the myths of consumer behavior that product designers tend to believe. Each chapter focuses on a different consumer behavior misconception by building a new, correct model for consumer behavior that more closely matches real consumers. This new model is described using graphical metaphors that help visualize how consumers behave relative to the myth. Finally, we give real-world examples or share our prior business intelligence results to demonstrate why the mythical practice should be avoided and how to succeed.

Myth 1:

Consumers behave the same in all markets

Reality:

Consumers behave differently in new markets than in established markets

Imagine the following fictitious conversation among the designers of the airplane phone during its early development:

"We have to be successful. Our market is just like that of the mobile phone. Look at its success!"

"Yes—in fact, we are an extension of the mobile phone. Now people can talk even while flying in a plane. Business people will use them on every flight!"

I travel on hundreds of flights every year and have seen only a few people use these phones. What went wrong?

The problem is that the makers and marketers of the airplane phone never thought to design and roll out their product as a *new* product. Instead, they expected their consumers to arrive committed and loyal, as if the airplane phone were already successful—maybe expecting consumers to see it as an extension to the mobile phone.

The reality is that users had to learn how to use, pay for, and accept the airplane phone. It *was* a young product and it had to go through the same growing pains all young products must endure. In hindsight, their enthusiasm to skip their growth phase and jump straight to success delayed the very success they coveted.

While it's not wrong to utilize other markets to learn how to succeed, it is wrong to assume consumers will interact the same with a new product as they do with a successful product. Learn how the successful product overcame its early consumer adoption hurdles, so you can overcome yours.

The *Consumer Adoption S-Curve*

The *Consumer Adoption S-Curve* will help clarify how markets transition from youth to maturity:

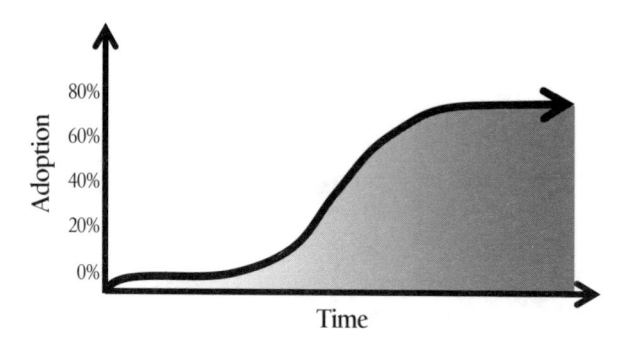

In this chart, the y-axis shows the percentage of users who have adopted the product, while the x-axis depicts time.

The *Consumer Adoption S-Curve* is the most commonly used—and misused—tool for comparing consumer markets. Few have truly mastered how to advance a new product through its life cycle. Entrepreneurs tend to assume that their product will automatically progress through the S-curve, causing them to salivate over the successes they'll soon have. Unfortunately, most products will never progress through this cycle, because the standard S-curve as drawn above only represents the best-case scenario, one that very few products will ever attain.

The S-curve can be broken down into three distinct phases:

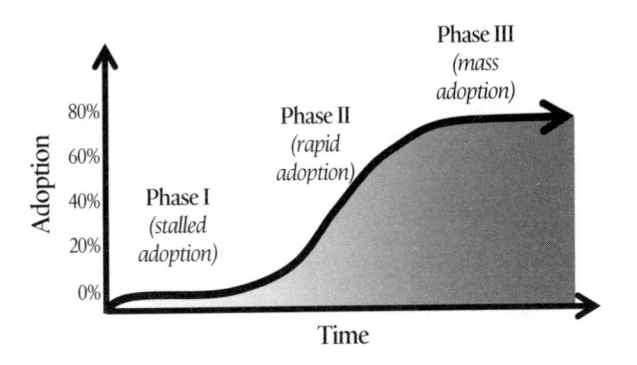

New products and services begin in Phase I, *stalled adoption*, and won't progress to Phase II, *rapid adoption*, until the product delivers consumer-grade usability and value. Phase II proceeds quickly because the barriers to adoption were removed in Phase I. To reach Phase III, *mass adoption*, both the product and its key competitive versions must be consumer grade.

The *Consumer Adoption S-Curve* is a great tool for comparing a new product or service to an established offering. Once you find a good comparison market, focus your energy on under-

standing its adoption transition from Phase I to Phase II—
what sparked rapid adoption growth? Any attempt to understand consumer behavior in later market phases is wishful
thinking at best. To achieve the growth and success of your
comparison market, you must copy its path, not its destina-
tion.

Progressing through the S-curve isn't simple, it isn't automatic,
and it isn't intuitive. If anything, the automatic behavior is for
products to *not* progress through the S-curve. Next, we describe each phase of the S-curve, showing how consumers behave and how you can react with both product changes and
marketing programs to maximize your success.

Phase I: Stalled adoption

Stalled adoption is caused by the product not being consumer
grade—either because the idea or product just doesn't have a
large enough consumer base or because it isn't usable by the
average consumer. Let's consider some common scenarios,
starting with an elongated Phase I:

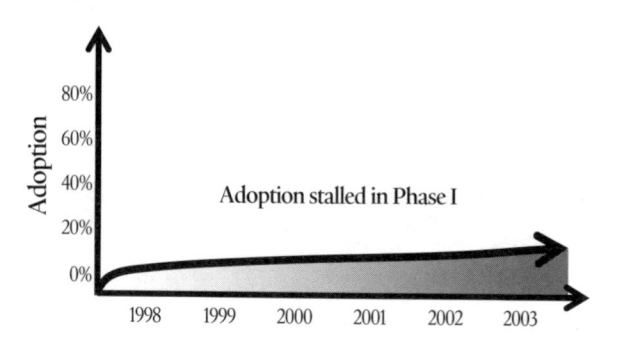

This example is for the European mobile Internet market,
which stalled in Phase I for nearly five years.

Even with the prolonged failure, the European mobile operators continued to invest in this market in the hope that they would achieve the success of the Japanese, who were having wild success with their market.

Earlier we mentioned how the airplane phone shouldn't be compared to the mobile phone because the mobile phone is in a mature market. In this case, comparing mobile Internet adoption in Europe and Japan, the products are the same, and so is the mistake, because the comparison is to the Japanese market, which is already successful.

Japan jumped through Phase I in 9 months:

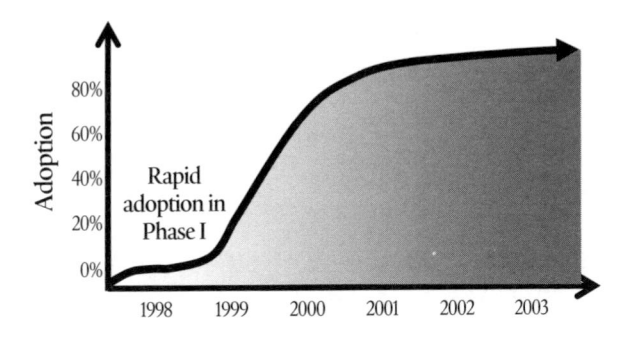

Why didn't adoption take off as quickly in Europe as it did in Japan? Why does the same product have two completely different S-curves in two different geographies? Clearly, there was a tremendous loss of revenue opportunity in Europe due to its inability to advance to Phase II adoption earlier.

Identifying barriers to entering Phase II

The answer lies in this chapter's reality: *Consumers behave differently in new markets than in established markets.* The European mobile phone operators failed to properly identify the barriers to Phase II (leaving them stuck in Phase I for years). Making Europe's plight worse—ironically—was Japan's success, which caused European operators to copy Japan's Phase III practices, hoping to skip their own Phases I and II. In some ways this helped, as it improved device capabilities in the region. But in many ways it slowed market growth, as the Europeans began charging for the same low-quality content that consumers weren't using when it was free. Phase III practices worked in Japan because the Japanese had a large addicted install base of users, but Japan didn't capture that install base by using Phase III practices—they did it by having quality, easy-to-use content and services that users fell in love with. The Europeans needed to copy the beginnings (great content), not the end (charging for content).

During Phase I it is critical that the offering be properly analyzed to find both its barriers to adoption and its keys to success. Barriers are often easily identified by employing the following methods:

Usability testing: Try testing your offering with real users to see how real consumers behave when using your features (we explain how to run usability tests in the last chapter, *How we can succeed*). It is quite sobering to watch real users struggle with your product. Find and fix these easy-to-find problems.

Business intelligence analysis: More simply put, analyze any data you have about your consumer usage, such as web logs or user purchase transactions. This allows you to see what is really happening "under the covers" and optimize based on consumer behavior patterns. We show many examples of business intelligence analysis in later chapters.

Best practice analysis: This is an introspective look at your product features and marketing activities to determine whether they are appropriate for the market (and market phase) you are in. In the case of new products and services (or new markets), best practices may not be established yet, and you should employ high-level practices like optimizing the speed of the service or reducing the number of steps in the service. Later, you can run usability tests and business intelligence analysis to reveal and refine the best practices specific to your offering or marketplace.

A good example of stalled adoption is the development of the original mobile phone market. It may be hard to believe, but at the original introduction of the mobile phone, it was not apparent whether this product would ever be successful. Consider how it stalled when it was in Phase I of the *Consumer Adoption S-Curve* and how the barriers had to be identified before it could progress to Phase II:

In 1983, the first commercial phone, the *DynaTAC 8000X*, was introduced by Motorola. It weighed 28 ounces (785 grams, which is the equivalent of 10 mobile phones today), was an incredible 13 inches tall, 3.5 inches high, and 1.75 inches wide ($300\times44\times89$mm); had only one hour of talk time and 8 hours of standby time (you needed 2 fully charged phones just to wait for calls during a normal day); and it cost the consumer $3,995. It had very limited coverage and was only purchased by very rich early adopters.[*]

Although 300,000 sold in the first year, it was 7 more years before the first 1,000,000 were sold, with the slow growth continuing for several more years (today 220 million mobile phones ship every quarter).[†] The implication here is that many

---

[*] From bbc.co.uk news article, *DynaTAC 8000X—the World's First Mobile Phone*, July 3, 2003.

[†] From IDC press release referencing IDC Worldwide Quarterly Mobile Phone Tracker, April 20, 2006.

early purchases were not repeat or loyal users. This growth and adoption performance was worse than that of the PDA of the 90s, and even worse than the PC of the 80s. Imagine that: The famously successful mobile phone—over a billion found worldwide today—*languished in Phase I adoption for over 10 years.*

Like any new product, the mobile phone had many consumer touch points, which were evaluated by each user at the time of purchase and provisioning. Users even had to evaluate when to use it, as in those days you didn't just make a mobile phone call—it was too expensive, the battery died very quickly, and the reception was miserable for both the caller and the callee.

To become consumer grade, mobile phone makers and operators had to discover what barriers prevented success and turn those barriers into *key success factors* that could be optimized. It ultimately took 10 years, but they eventually identified the success factors as coverage, reception quality, size, weight, and battery life. This paved the road for the mobile phone to find massive consumer success.

What if this is a new service? How do we find the best practices, hidden barriers, and key success factors? Try analyzing these areas:

Purchasing and first-use barriers: If you are introducing a new paradigm to replace an older, less efficient solution to a problem, then make sure you don't also introduce new costs or usage barriers to trying that solution. Users will almost always choose an old method rather than jump through new hoops—even common hoops like registration—to try a new solution. The best services have zero extra steps to turning on the service and trying it. Save your registration screens and new pricing programs until after the market starts growing.

Hidden value: New solutions are supposed to provide value. Every step the user takes to find that value (including looking for that value) will drastically reduce the number of users who ultimately find and use the feature. Identify what your value is and make sure your user will find it with no intermediate steps.

Poor performance: Most users won't notice poor performance when they first try a new product or service, but the second or third time they use it they will. Users who become wary of the slowness will simply stop using the product, or stop returning for the service.

Poor usability: Is it easy to find the value of the product on the first use? Is it easy to return to that value in the future?

Poor market segmentation: Too many companies want to jump directly to Phase III adoption, with every user in every market segment using their service. Ultimately, the product or idea may support this, but initially consumers need specific reasons to try your product. While some market segments may show greater early interest than others, broadening the segmentation too early can obscure the product's value in all segments.

Now let's take another look at the airplane phone and see whether we can spot the consumer barriers:

The makers of airplane phones probably thought they had the next major consumer hit. Given the incredible success of mobile phones, they likely thought that they would have a huge user base—after all, who doesn't want to be connected?

Furthermore, they figured they have a few extra points to their advantage compared to consumer mobile phones. First, a large percentage of fliers are businesspeople, and they are already addicted to the gadgets of their mobile lifestyle, such as mobile phones. Second, fliers are more affluent than the average consumer, so the extra cost shouldn't be an issue. Finally, purchase of the phone is not required to use the service. What riches must have been projected!

Here we are, many years later, and you might see one person using these phones for every 20–30 flights, even though there is a phone within reach of every passenger. Almost no one uses this service.

What went wrong? Why didn't this market automatically take off?

The problem is that this service is designed as if its users already accept it and does little or nothing to help them through the evaluation period (and even less to keep them once they try it). By failing to properly study their consumers' behaviors, they wasted millions of dollars outfitting planes and networks.

Even though consumers are familiar with making phone calls, airplane phones have plenty of barriers to use:

First, airplane phone use is not intuitive. Landline phones give you a dial tone, and then you dial. Mobile phones require you to dial, then hit send. Airplane phones do neither. Do I have to swipe a credit card, then dial? Or do I dial, then swipe? Do I go through a menu on the display first?

Next, these phones appear to be expensive—after all, they require a credit card, and consumers are conditioned to use credit cards only for purchases over $20. Also, businesspeople do have extra discretionary allowances, but only if they can easily expense the item after the trip. Airplane phones don't give a receipt that can be easily used for reimbursements.

Finally, what about usability? The tethering line (cord) to the phone is awkward, not to mention the phone's blocky shape. It can be minutes before the call is connected, and it is unclear whether you can use these while taxiing or during takeoffs and landings (or do I have to wait for the plane to get airborne? How long do I wait? How high do we need to be?). Finally, you can't walk away from others when you need privacy (like with a mobile phone)—your airplane conversation stays public from start to finish.

The airplane phone is a new paradigm, with a new set of issues to be discovered and optimized before it can become a consumer grade solution. What do their vendors do about this? Focus only on price (an ill-advised marketing attempt to attract more users; see Myth 2) or Internet access (more features; see Myth 5). What about all of the other consumer barriers listed above?

This market is doomed to stay in Phase I until the key adoption barriers are properly identified and optimized out.

Fueling adoption in Phase II

Once you get to Phase II adoption, you must begin fueling its growth. This is when it is appropriate to start developing additional market segments. Moving from Phase I into Phase II is such a monumental effort that, once you get there, it will be obvious what the key attributes of success are. In Phase II these success factors must continue to be optimized for your initial market segment while expanding to other similar market segments (don't take your eyes off the ball).

Business intelligence analysis is the best way to spot new market segments and to develop them. Looking closely at the usage patterns of your service will tell you who is driving usage, who is following, and what they are doing. Without business intelligence analysis of your usage patterns, you are guessing in three ways:

You are guessing which segment to grow: You don't know, for example, whether the business market will lead or follow the youth market. You may not even know which market is driving your Phase II success.

You are guessing at your success: How will you know if this new segment is taking hold properly unless you analyze the usage patterns to spot this new segment's growth?

You are risking your original customer base: How do you know if your new focus is hurting your original customer base?

Another phenomenon of Phase II growth is that it can stall, making your S-curve look like this:

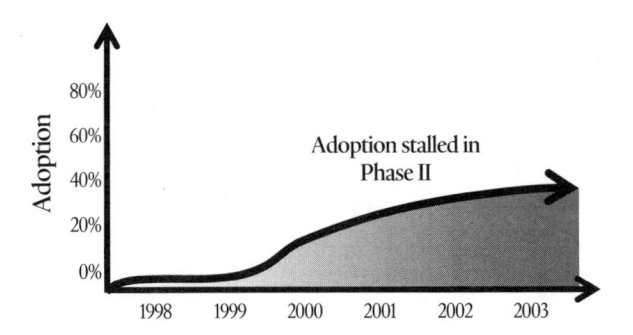

Usually, stalling in Phase II is caused by one of three things:

Lack of business intelligence: Your company isn't properly analyzing its usage patterns and growing the correct market segments quickly.

Lack of quality competition: The competition is locked in Phase I and they have enough market share to prevent the entire market from spurring a lifestyle change, thus slowing down your company's growth as well.

Early rush to focus on per user revenue: Focusing too early on ARPU (average revenue per user) is a big killer in Phase II. The proper growth process is to first grow revenue by adding new users (building the install base). Jumping to an ARPU-centric model too early in Phase II (or, heaven forbid, in Phase I) will narrow your consumer base to only those who have already become fully addicted at the time of transition. ARPU focus usually means extra charges for use, which is an insurmountable barrier for new users.

In summary:

Find and analyze all available consumer data

Continue to optimize your key success factors

Don't jump too quickly to a focus on ARPU

Garner enough positive industry press so that your competitors will copy you enough to keep the market growing.

Don't worry about competitors taking away your market share, as you will also establish yourself as the market leader and will continue to own the lion's share of the market.

Make more money per user in Phase III

So you have a strong addicted install base. If you are really in Phase III, you have created a lifestyle change with your product, just as the Internet, DVD, or MP3 player once did. When you are in Phase III, most people on the street know the value of your product or service, know how to operate it, and are addicted to it.

What can you do with addicted users that you can't readily do with a "ho-hum" install base? Make more money. Usually this comes through incremental improvements users will now pay for. Your users are addicted, and they will welcome more value even at higher cost. You cannot grow revenue by growing the install base anymore, so you must vary the product offering with more purchasing or upgrade options, more up-sell opportunities, and more refinements. Whereas Phase I and Phase II consumers would have never accepted these changes, this added complexity is absorbed readily by your install base now that they are addicted.

You have to be careful here, because your competition should also be entering Phase III of adoption. If they feel you are the leader, they will usually drop their price to attack your market share. The only victor of a price war is the end user—and then maybe even only temporarily, because loss of margins translates into lower investments on future developments and quality. Ensuring that your proposition is the most attractive helps retain value—and helps prevent your service from being treated as a commodity.

Different practices are needed in different phases

There are clearly three phases of consumer adoption, and consumer behavior is drastically different in each phase. The most important difference between new markets and established markets is that of how consumers behave when addicted to a product versus trying a new one. Established markets have motivated consumers and permit completely different allowable practices.

Below is a table that highlights the negative or positive reaction consumers will have to different practices at different S-curve phases:

Practice	Phase I	Phase II	Phase III
Broad market segmentation	−		+
Multi-tiered pricing strategy	−		+
Heavy marketing investment	−	+	+
Great usability	+	+	
Great performance	+	+	
Optimizing key success factors	+	+	+
Focus on ARPU	−	−	+

Note: A minus sign "−" means that consumers respond negatively to the practice, a blank means it makes little difference, and a plus sign "+" means consumers will react positively to the practice.

Now let's return to the difference between the European and Japanese markets for mobile Internet. Both markets sell the same product, but the Japanese market went through Phase I in 9 months, while the Europeans took several years.

In Japan, you can purchase anything on your phone—from perfume to subway tickets to Disneyland rides—and these purchases add up to additional ARPU for the operators. Japan's users not only put up with this additional cost, they like it—it feeds their addiction.

The European's saw this happening and started charging for different content on their mobile phones. They failed to consider that their small base of ho-hum users wouldn't pay for something they barely tolerated when it was free. Furthermore, why would a new user tolerate extra purchasing barriers while trying to learn about the new service? How do you get addicted users from consumers who are not interested? Surely, it isn't by raising the price!

Analysis of Phase I in Japan shows a brief period of stalled adoption. Both NTT DoCoMo and KDDI offered a broad spectrum of Internet sites to browse, like personal banking, directory services, stock quotes, news, sports, weather, and messaging. But consumers didn't use these types of services, and it soon looked like a total failure. Japanese operators struggled to get users to return.

The Japanese carriers studied the few early adopters to determine what they were using, striving to find what was working. Soon they identified one service that had more repeat usage than any other: Mobile e-mail.

Wasting no time, operators rushed to optimize mobile e-mail to make it easier to use (fewer key clicks, automatic pop-up messages when e-mail arrived, simpler provisioning at point of purchase, faster client versions, local storage for messages, a dedicated key for launching e-mail, etc.). Within 9 months of their initial launch, new phones were shipping that delivered on the market's demonstrated need, and the delivery was consumer grade.

Soon every user in Japan who bought a mobile phone found e-mail one button press away, and they found that sending and receiving e-mails to and from their friends was beyond simple. More and more users became more and more addicted, and the market grew rapidly.

In Europe, however, the mobile Internet went through a completely different cycle because they bought into Myth 1, rather than countering it.

The mobile Internet market started out rocky for the Europeans. Instead of viewing their market as that of a new technology product in Phase I adoption, they viewed their market as an extension of another successful market—the Internet on the PC.

Thus, they marketed the service with the marketing message, "Internet on the Phone," and set up web sites like those popular on the PC.

This immediately set up many failure points. First, their marketing of Internet access from the phone led new consumers to undelivered value. This was an unrealistic and unobtainable experience (how do you surf the Internet on your phone, with a small screen and no keyboard?). Users also didn't understand why they needed mobile Internet access. Why replace a perfect experience with a mediocre one?

The content providers, unfortunately, fell into this trap as well, implementing PC Internet concepts (creating extremely poor versions of their PC web applications on the phone, which had at that time only a few lines of display and no graphics). Who wants to perform 75 key-clicks and spend 4½ minutes to get a stock quote on a phone? To make a bad situation worse, most European sites required users to register first from the phone. If you have ever tried to enter your full name, create a user name and password, or enter your e-mail address on a phone's triple-tap keyboard, you know why few users would fill out a form or log on to a site from the phone.

The European operator's market blunder (Internet on the phone), coupled with their rush to copy the Japanese and charge for services that nobody was using even when they were free, put the brakes on this market. It had no chance of growth because it tried to skip Phase I adoption and ignored consumer behavior.

In this case, early marketing of the wrong key value and marketing an undeliverable service contributed greatly to the poor initial experiences and low consumer adoption in Europe. Ultimately, this drew out Phase I adoption for many years, whereas in Japan Phase I lasted only 9 months. It wasn't until 2003 when Vodafone introduced *Vodafone live!*—focused on services the Europeans were really using—that mobile Internet started to take off in Europe.

Conclusion: New markets are different

Adding a feature or changing a practice based on comparisons with an established market is not a good idea. Poor comparisons with the wrong market, or the right market in a different phase of the S-curve, will cripple your own product's success. Don't fall into the trap unless you can truly differentiate your market's key success factors from the one you are copying, and unless you can copy the other market's Phase I growth practices. No product has ever skipped its own growth phases, but many dollars have been wasted trying.

Bottom line: *New users won't behave the same as addicted users.* Measure, analyze, and optimize until you find your product's key success factors and then fine-tune those attributes until consumers start adopting your product. Analyze the product or service with a focus on finding problems, not on justifying prior decisions. It is often easier to contract consultants for this work, as they will spot problems without the blinders of historical decision-making and politics.

However you identify the problems, remember that your company is responsible for making the changes. Fix your product to make it work better for its consumers. Don't expect consumers to change their behavior for your product—they won't.

Myth 2:

The more consumers see it, the more successful it will be

Reality:

If the offering isn't attractive, there is no point in getting more users to see it

A common muttering of the engineering team after a product begins to languish in the marketplace:

"We need more marketing. Nobody knows about it. The product won't sell itself. Users will love it once they see it!"

Of course, they are right—you need to attract users to your product—but, typically, the real problem with most products is keeping users interested. Consumers won't use a product they don't find useful. No amount of marketing will make a bad product good in the eyes of a consumer.

Promotions aren't effective until the product or service can effectively convert its users into long-term customers. Not everyone who tries a product will *stick* with it. In fact, most people *bounce off* new technology products even before they find the real value. The *Consumer Adoption Funnel* is used to measure and observe this consumer behavior phenomenon.

The *Consumer Adoption Funnel*

Users don't fall in love with a new product instantly. Instead, they transition from a disinterested potential user into a loyal user by passing through several levels of acceptance, each level introducing a new gate or barrier that each user will have to pass through successfully in order to reach the next level. These gates are collectively the *Consumer Adoption Funnel*,[‡] which is like a sieve that restricts the number of users who become regular addicted users:

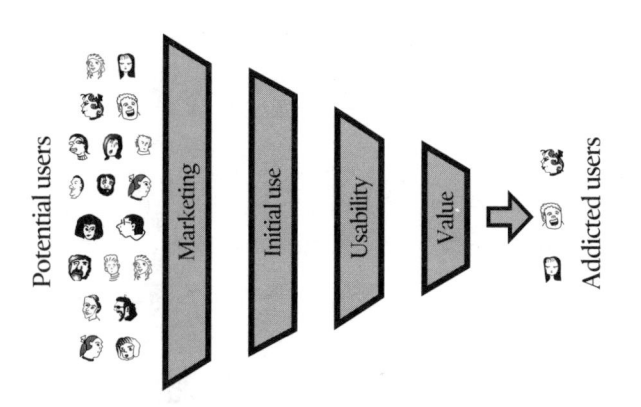

[‡] Note that it's called a funnel because of its shape—gradually getting smaller from one end to the other. It's not like a real funnel, where everything that you put in comes out the other end. If all potential users really came out the other end, this job would be easy. We'll stick with a funnel, because it's a well-understood concept.

Getting users to try the product

The first gate in the *Consumer Adoption Funnel* is marketing, and the goal is to get the maximum number of users to try your product or service. The more noise you make, the more users you will attract:

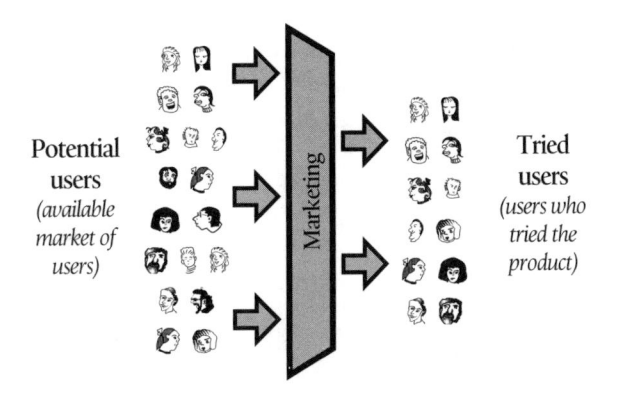

This splits users into two categories:

Potential users: This is the available market. If this is a broad-based consumer technology product, like television, the Internet, or mobile phones, then this includes all users in the geographic area where the product is sold. This will be a subset of the population if the product is for a more limited audience.

Tried users: These are the users who have attempted to try the product or service. It is a subset all potential users. Not every user who tries the product succeeds at getting the product to work.

The marketing gate represents all outbound marketing activities that are used to entice users to try the product, including programs such as the following:

Public relations: Using the press and industry to gain support for your product is the best way to attract users, as a consumer's optimism is at its highest after reading a good review on your product. Consumers trust this advice to be independent and unbiased.

Advertising: This is the most obvious way to entice users to try your product, but it is also the most expensive. Furthermore, just as consumers behave with optimism to a good review, they behave with skepticism when they read your advertisements.

Branding: Users behave better to branding if the branding targets a narrow enough segment of the market for consumers to want to include themselves in this group, allowing them to also include themselves in your product's community or image. This lowers skepticism and can help attract users to try the product.

Pricing: Lowering the price can also attract users, as this lowers the barriers to trying the product. Pricing is important in Phase I adoption because cost can be a barrier, but sometimes lowering the price too much also becomes a barrier. A very inexpensive product implies the product has low value, low quality, or is useless. *Cheap* is not a good brand image.

Retail experience: If the product, such as PCs and mobile phones, is sold in a retail setting, then the retail channel personnel can be given incentives to entice users to try the product or to use the product in new ways.

To the engineers in our earlier example, this single segment of the *Consumer Adoption Funnel* is the entire marketing landscape. Marketing attracts users and everything is successful, right? Reality shows that there are more barriers...

"Initial use" is a barrier

Once users are attracted to the product, they go through the next gate in the *Consumer Adoption Funnel*, which is where they try to get the product to work for them:

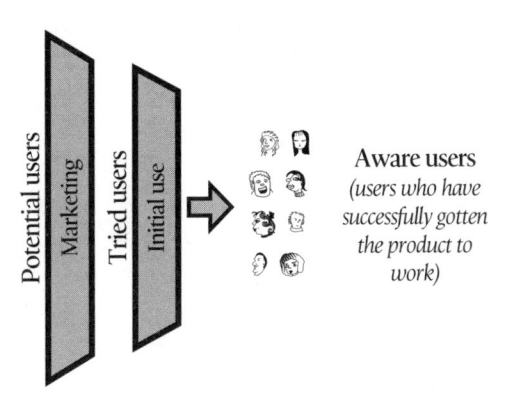

Aware users
(users who have successfully gotten the product to work)

The fact that *initial use* reduces the number of users is often a surprise to most companies. The reality is that significantly fewer users actually get the product to work for them than companies are willing to accept.

Consider this example of an Internet site we analyzed for a client (the name will be left out since this example highlights their failure as much as their success):

> We were hired to perform a business intelligence analysis of an Internet site that offered a service directed at a broad consumer market. When we completed the analysis, we found two interesting facts: (1) The company had attracted over 2,500,000 users to their site over the previous six months; and (2) less than 8% of those users actually found the key features of the product (the rest gave up). Put another way, 92% of the users who tried didn't succeed, and therefore were very unlikely to return and become addicted.

Going against the advice of this myth, and against the consumer behavior we were able to prove through factual analysis, the company offering the service issued a press release showing off its "success" in "a large user base." This company ignored the negative news (most users were not finding value or using the product long term), and their funnel continued to deteriorate over time. By counting tried users as real users, this company delayed its growth to Phase II of consumer adoption by over 3 years.

Below is a list of common barriers that users encounter in their first experimental use of products and services:

Provisioning: Provisioning is the process of setting up back-end delivery systems and infrastructure to "know" and accept a new user. For example, a company that hosts e-mail for consumers needs to properly set up their back-end e-mail server with your default information before you can start receiving e-mail. Since most consumers won't understand what provisioning is or why it is needed, this step should be minimized or eliminated— new users should be able to try the service without any hassles.

Consider this example of a broken provisioning system for the mobile phone:

One major operator we consulted with provided mobile Internet service on every mobile phone sold. However, to try the service, users had to first call the operator and subscribe to the service. Only after that could they click on the Internet feature in their phone. If they clicked on the feature before changing service plans, they got an error message.

Looked at from a user's viewpoint, you have a phone you bought to make phone calls, and eventually you see the Internet button and decide to give it a try. You click on this button and get a failure message "Service unavailable." Of course, this tells you that your phone doesn't support the feature, so you never try again (or you try, but always fail).

The message "Service unavailable" came from an infrastructure component in the service provider's network that needed to be provisioned for every new user before they could use the Internet service. It failed because the consumer didn't proactively call the operator and sign up for the service in advance. Clearly, the message could have been better, like "Please call support for access to this feature," but even then only a small population would be motivated to make that phone call—especially since it means signing up to pay for something they don't even know is valuable.

Two simple solutions to this problem would be to either provision all users automatically to a plan that offered free access for the first month or to charge per access until users change their service options. Once addicted, users could then opt to select a more economical plan.

Registration: It is common for Internet web sites to require users to register before they can gain deeper access to the services. Most users won't commit to giving away personal information just to see what a web site offers, so don't require registration until after the user is able to see the value of the service. If a user name is required as part of the basic operation (e.g., e-mail), keep this registration process to a bare minimum. Don't burden new users with requirements to try a new service.

Installation: Installation is a necessity for software applications on the PC and Macintosh. However, this doesn't mean that this process is well understood by all consumers. In fact, most consumers will take whatever defaults the installation program offers (so don't burden

average users with your power-user installation options).
One-step installation is critical.

Consider television installation as an example:

> What would you think of a television that required
> you to set the clock, tune the channels, set the color
> environment, set the brightness, etc., before you could
> watch your first program? You wouldn't be very
> happy with that TV.

> In the U.K. this isn't uncommon. This is also becoming
> common in the U.S., with the introduction of
> high-definition TVs. Most consumers will take what-
> ever default the TV gives them, and most won't spend
> hours adjusting a TV before watching it the first time.

> Consider two examples, one Ali, the coauthor of this
> book, gives from the U.K., and the other an experience
> I had in the U.S. (in a twist, the U.K. example will
> show how to do it right, even though it is uncommon
> for televisions to work out-of-the box there; whereas
> my experience in the U.S.—where it used to be done
> right—demonstrates how new products can, unfortu-
> nately, reintroduce a bad experience):

> Ali bought his television, connected it up to the aerial,
> and turned it on. He expected to be presented with a
> bunch of setup screens, but to his surprise a message
> appeared on the screen that said "I'm tuning—please
> wait." Within a couple of minutes the television had
> selected the strongest signals available for the five
> channels available in the U.K., set its clock, and pro-
> grammed all the channels in a logical order—bingo.

> Now for my example. I bought my high-definition TV
> in the U.S. in 2000. I always assumed that I was
> watching high-definition (since the screen was good
> and big), but I wasn't impressed. During a holiday in
> 2004 I decided to look closer and found that the fancy

and very expensive high-definition TV I bought hadn't played a single high-definition program over the past four years (its default behavior was to *not* play high definition!). It took over a week for me to figure out how to turn the high-definition feature on and get a signal that played high-definition on a few specific channels. I can't begin to explain my frustration and disappointment.

Setup: Many products will ask you to set up preferences before using it. This is different from installation (a step to making it work) and different from registration (as it only relates to the user's environment, not access to their personal information). This step should be avoided or eliminated.

The mobile Internet presents some good examples:

There are many mobile Internet services that allow you to fully customize their environment, which is usually done to help work around the constraints of the environment (small screen, limited keypad, etc.).

One site we evaluated required all new users to go through a process of selecting their preferences before using the service. Therefore, whenever a new user tried it, a series of screens asking questions like where they live (so it could provide weather), what their favorite sports are (so they could provide that sport on the homepage), etc., appeared.

By looking at the transactions to this site, we noticed immediately that, although the site had a high attraction rate (meaning many users desired to use it), only a very small percentage of the new users (12% in this case) got through the setup process and on to the value of that service.

Users are not in the proper state of mind to go through setup steps to optimize a product or service before they can see what that service does. Consumers view extra setup steps as complexity, and when exploring a new product, the last thing consumers want is a complex experience.

Navigation: Don't hide your value (described further in Myth 4). Since 80–90% of new users will usually want the same basic features, key features need to be differentiated early on in navigation paths.

The best way to handle the initial use gate is to optimize out every possible decision or step that delays users from finding the product's most valuable feature. Business intelligence is a great tool for isolating these drop-off points, as well as helping to determine where the true value is (i.e., where most users go to and return to again later).

Usability is a barrier

The next gate that reduces the number of users is the product's inherent usability and performance:

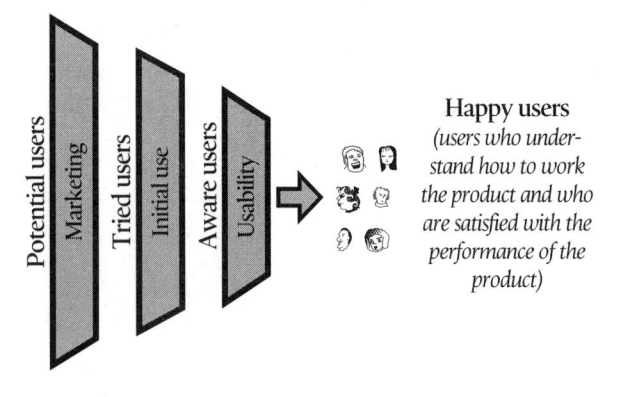

Potential users · Marketing · Tried users · Initial use · Aware users · Usability

Happy users
(users who understand how to work the product and who are satisfied with the performance of the product)

Just because a user has figured out how to get your product to work (i.e., they passed through the "initial use" gate), doesn't mean they will want to use that product over the long term. Users often find that usability issues or poor performance is too great to make it worth returning to and using the product again.

Common usability problems include:

Performance: How fast is your product? If the user is trying to use the product 5 times a day, then the product better produce a valuable result in a few seconds. Would you accept a TV that takes 5 minutes to boot up? You need to find the performance drop-off of users (i.e., the point where users give up on your product because it is too slow) and optimize your service or product to ensure that it operates inside this envelope.

Confusing labels or directions: It is amazing how little effort people give to labels, like software menu labels or button labels. Often the help provided is as bad as the original label.

Let's look at an example I had with DVD-playing software I bought for my laptop:

I got a new laptop computer with a built-in DVD player and quickly found that the quality of the sound was preventing me from enjoying it. I searched on the Internet to see what solutions would work and found that there were companies that sold software packages for playing DVDs that would (they said) perform better at many tasks, one of them even with an audio booster package that looked like it would solve the problem.

So I purchased and downloaded the software, installed it, and got it working—great. But the audio was still lousy. No problem—I'll just boost the audio performance through its settings.

I went through the setup boxes until I found a screen related to audio, where I found a checkbox that said: "Use Hardware Decode Acceleration." This box wasn't checked, and I wondered why. The system had made an initial decision to have this off, but it sounded like a good thing to me. I had no idea what "Hardware Decode Acceleration" means (this is a very techie label to present to a consumer), but I wanted to make sure I set everything up correctly.

Why wasn't this feature checked? There is no context-sensitive help (which usually doesn't help anyway, as it usually says something like "If you want Hardware Decode Acceleration, then check this box"—which just demonstrates to me that the person who wrote it doesn't know what it means either).

It took me 20 minutes to find an online manual and the explanation within the online manual for this feature. It said: "Enable Use Hardware Decode Acceleration to ensure that the DVD player uses the hardware motion compensation provided by your VGA card." Great, that really clears things up (not!). Why was it turned off? Will turning it on break my computer? How would I possibly know if my VGA card supports this? (It is a laptop, so I don't even know if such a card exists.) Useless!

You need to know how consumers interpret your main screens and messages. It is worth running a usability test to see how users perceive your text and how well they follow directions. Most issues derive from the company assuming consumers have the same deep understanding of its technology as they do (like the example above, where the DVD technology is beyond me, the average consumer, who just wants to play a movie with the best possible performance and quality).

Too many steps: What is the key value of your product or service (i.e., what is the one feature that every user wants to use and returns to the most)? Now count the number of steps it takes to get to that value. Is it zero? If not, you should spend all of your time trying to get it to zero. Likewise, you should determine how much time it takes for a consumer to find that feature (like in a usability study). If it takes more than a few seconds for a new user to find the value, you can bet most won't find it (see Myth 4).

Let's look at some PC products for examples on how to eliminate steps:

> It is no accident that when you launch Microsoft Word you get an empty document, with the ability to open recent documents on a panel on the side, or that when you launch your e-mail program you get your inbox. These programs understand their value and make sure it is seen first.

> When Internet e-mail became available, I chose Hotmail for my personal e-mail because it allowed me to get to my inbox with the fewest steps. Logging in was always one mouse-click away since it remembered my user account and password.

> Yahoo! e-mail, on the other hand, refused to remember my password for longer than a few days and required two more screens before I got to my inbox (it says this is for security). Instead of just clicking once with the mouse, I had to type my password all the time and had to navigate through the extra screens.

> Hotmail could have eliminated one screen by starting me in my inbox, like Microsoft Outlook, but the fact

that I didn't have to type my user name and password made it better for me, with the many times I have to check my e-mail each day.

These extra steps become important to regular users—they won't accept unproductive barriers every time they use a product. Imagine if Microsoft Outlook came up with a dialog every time you used it and asked if you wanted to compose a new e-mail, look at your inbox, or look in other folders? You would select to look at your inbox 99% of the time, and you would never understand why it didn't start there in the first place (which is why it does start there).

Hard to learn/remember: Users want to focus on the task or value of the product or service, not the user interface. It is your job to reduce and simplify until this is possible.

Consider MS DOS and the transition to Windows:

> The fundamental difference between features in programs written for MS DOS and Windows is the amount of training required to use the product the first time and the amount of remembering required to continue to use the software later.

> During the transition from MS DOS to Windows, companies diverted most of their engineering resources to recreate their old MS DOS features in the Windows environment. This took so much time that most programs were released in Windows with only a subset of their MS DOS features. To further cripple the Windows versions of these programs, the Windows environment required more from the hardware, causing its programs to run slower and use more memory (leaving less memory for the user's tasks or documents).

> So, with fewer features in Windows, running slower than their MS DOS counterparts, and with less mem-

ory to maneuver, most experts at the time expected the Windows programs to fail. Nevertheless, when all was said and done, users preferred Windows because it was easier to learn and remember. The extra features, speed, and capacity available in MS DOS were secondary to the usability provided by Windows.

This lesson needs to be taken to heart because learning how to use new products is a real barrier. Windows, by imposing consistency on developers, made applications generally much easier to learn. Although the developers may have thought they could do better, those who took that consistent approach were more successful in the end.

Too many decisions: How many decisions do your users have to make before they get to the value of your product or service? Consumers don't want to make decisions; they want the product to work "out of the box."

Even minor decisions provide an opportunity for users to defect:

> To the product designer, a simple binary question posed to a user can have only two answers, such as "Go left" or "Go right," but to the user there are three possible answers: "Go left," "Go right," and "Give up"—and, unfortunately, "Give up" moves closer to the top of the decision tree every time another question is asked.

We once evaluated a Chat program for a major Internet provider and found that 50,000 users had tried the Chat program during the week we analyzed. This was the good news. The bad news was that we could only account for 13,000 users actually finding value.

The problems began when users first entered the Chat program, where they were given a legal disclosure warning that the company wasn't responsible for what people posted. Next, the user had to sign in with a user name. Finally, the user got a menu of different categories of chat boards. Only after selecting a chat board would the user receive value from the service.

The first screen, the legal disclosure, need only be accepted to continue, yet 50% of the users quit at this point, leaving only 24,000 users going forward.

The login screen, where the user established a "handle" or user name for posting messages, weeded out another 50% of users. Of the original 50,000 users, only 13,000 users got to the main menu, where they could then select a message board to view.

This meant that 13,000 users still hadn't found the value (the value of Chat is to view other people's messages within a board, not get to the main menu). This was a disaster.

The fix, once the facts were known, was fairly easy.

First, the operator made the legal notice permanently dismissible, meaning users could check a box to request that it not appear in the future (most users did).

Next, the login was eliminated from the beginning of the program—why log in just to read messages or see who is on the boards? The login was held back until it was required for a transaction, such as posting a message. This allowed users to browse message boards and read messages first (which helped greatly to get new users hooked). This was also better for the user's state of mind, as a user who is motivated enough to post a message for all the world to see on a public message board is not concerned about logging in. In this case, the user's state of mind and the activity are synchronized.

All of these improvements helped most users get closer to success quicker with this application.

The final two changes we suggested were too difficult for the next version. We recommended that the system recognize users as they entered so that they would never have to type in their user name, and we suggested the system remember the user's favorite message board so it could drop users directly to that board when they entered the Chat service.

Even without the final two changes, the company reported back to us that they had a 300% increase in usage after making the other product enhancements.

Too many repeat steps: Even if the user can navigate through the product to get to the value, how many steps do they have to repeat every time they use it?

The example about Yahoo! requiring me to type in my password every time I used it is a great example of too many repeat steps, and it is the primary reason I chose their competitor's product, Hotmail. Also, when I want to address a user in Hotmail, I click on a button of common users. In Yahoo! I had to go through a series of windows and pages to perform this same step.

Hotmail seems to respect my time and effort, whereas Yahoo! e-mail seems more concerned with the fact that the feature exists and works rather than with usability or performance.

Too many features: Too many features are actually a bad thing for a Phase I product. When new users are trying to understand what your product does and to answer the question, "Is it for me?" you need to sacrifice features, not add more of them. The success of Google over Yahoo! as an Internet search engine is a good example of this:

Sacrifice has clearly helped Google beat Yahoo! Google appears to offer only one feature (search). Yahoo!'s site, on the other hand, bombards users with dozens of features. Eventually, as we all know today, Google won the search engine war.

As a footnote, Yahoo!, in their "add more features" culture and in direct opposition to why they were losing, licensed the Google search engine. To say the least, this feature switch-out had little measurable effect on Yahoo!'s slide in this critical market (and proves that it wasn't the technology that determined the market share).

Feature overload is such an important point that Myth 5 is dedicated to it.

Confusing navigation: If the user can't readily find a feature due to complex navigation, they will likely fail and stop using the product.

I've seen this problem most often in the mobile Internet, where users find features through menus rather than by clicking on links. Ask a user in a usability test to find, for example, a weather report for their region and you will usually see him make dozens of navigational mistakes, such as thinking he will find it in News or Information.

Test your navigational paths and make sure your key features don't require users to memorize a complex navigational scheme.

Ugly layouts: This is probably the only area where usability becomes more of an Art than a Science (most of usability can actually be proven through testing and business intelligence). Ugly layouts can confuse the user and lower the perceived quality of the product.

The best use of artistic design to attract users is the Apple Macintosh or Apple iPod. These beautiful designs and simple applications are extremely appealing to most consumers.

Both of these products used their designs to make themselves approachable by novice consumers. Many would argue that the personal computer revolution wouldn't have happened if Macintosh hadn't first simplified and beautified the user interface (and Microsoft duplicated that success).

Similarly, the iPod turned a techie term, "MP3," into a major consumer market, where consumers could own an attractive player and easily download music without hassles from the same manufactures (at iTunes).

What is the value?

Now we can complete the *Consumer Adoption Funnel*. The last gate that prevents users from using a product or service is the amount of value it offers:

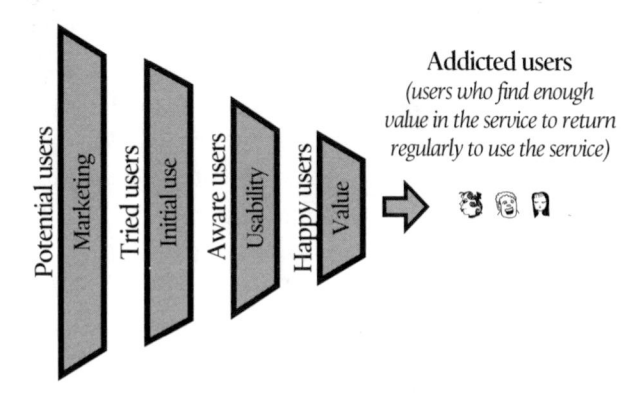

It is common for value to evaporate from a product as the product evolves during its development. The process of losing value typically flows like this:

First, the problem is identified: Fundamentally, every new consumer technology product or service begins with a great idea, one that usually represents a solution to a consumer problem.

A feature is born: The inventor usually imagines a solution to the problem and then labels that solution with a name like "listen to music while exercising." This label is reduced down to a feature, like "mobile music," as it is implemented.

The feature morphs: To implement the feature, many decisions, tradeoffs, and modifications must occur. After months or even years, the first version of the product is introduced to the market. In our example of "mobile music," this may mean creating the original gadget to play the music, including hardware, battery life, and storage.

Finally, the problem is lost: This is the unfortunate part of the story. While focusing on implementing the *feature* of "mobile music," the team forgot the original problem of "listening to music while exercising." In the worst case, the lost information about the problem can cause the feature to evolve into an implementation that prevents consumers from solving the original problem. The value is lost from the feature. For example, what if the first player introduced shorts out if exposed to perspiration?

The only way to truly measure *value* is to compare it against *cost*, as consumers do. Cost is the amount of effort or money it takes to solve a problem or get to the value. Consumers won't use a product if the cost is greater than the value.

Look at it as a seesaw, with *cost* on one side, *value* on the other, and users evaluating the difference in the middle:

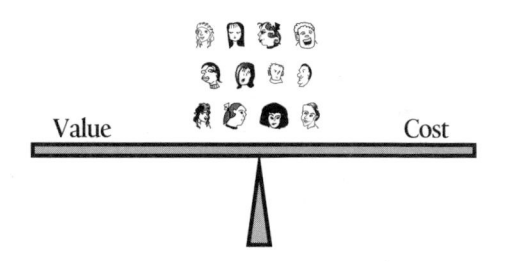

If your value is greater than the cost, then many users will use your product:

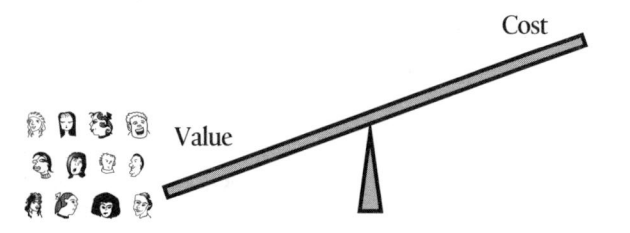

However, if your cost is greater than your value, you will find few users willing to use your product:

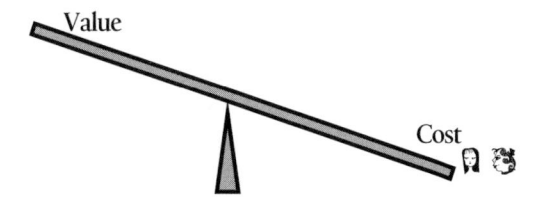

This chapter has already outlined most of the common costs consumers face as they migrate through the *Consumer Adoption Funnel*'s initial use gate and usability gate.

Here are these common costs listed again:

Initial use costs	Usability costs
(costs to try the product)	*(costs to use the product)*
Pricing	Performance
Provisioning	Confusing labels
Registration	Too many steps
Install	Hard to learn/remember
Setup	Too many decisions
Navigation	Too many repeat steps
	Too expensive
	Too many features
	Confusing navigation
	Ugly layouts

Notice that the actual financial cost of the product isn't the only cost to trying or using a new product or service. There are many hidden opportunity costs that will often have greater influence on a product's success than its monetary cost.

It usually comes as a shock to businesspeople that even something that is free may have too high a cost to the end user. Consider a personal experience I had using two different products to make Internet phone calls (one that has a monthly charge of $15; the other one, free):

> My first experience was with a product called Skype, which is a free service for making phone calls using the Internet. Since I am constantly traveling around the world I was excited that I might be able to communicate with my wife less expensively (I bought into their

marketing). I was motivated to get this product to work and I was willing to put up with all kinds of hassles.

So I downloaded and installed Skype on both my wife's computer and my laptop. I bought two top-of-the-line USB headsets with microphones, spending over $50 each (so much for "free"). I provisioned an account for my wife and me with Skype and soon got the system working from home. The connections were intuitive, and the sound quality, while not great, was bearable.

Next, I tried using it from the road. This failed. At home we have DSL, which is pretty fast. In Europe, I was stuck using modems most of the time, and when I did find Wi-Fi or high-speed Internet in a hotel, it really wasn't very fast. The sound quality was so bad and delayed that it wasn't worth using. After aborting several calls with my wife we agreed it wasn't worth using.

But since I paid so much for those fancy headsets I continued trying to make phone calls from my computer whenever possible. At the time, my colleagues were experimenting with Skype, so we all agreed to use its service for business phone calls to each other.

Soon I discovered why Skype was free. It crashed my computer several times a day, usually while trying to connect to a colleague for a phone call. We had to make landline phone calls constantly to talk to each other while trying to fix broken Skype calls. After a couple of weeks we all decided to stop using the service.

Stopping wasn't enough. My wife's Skype number got published in the Skype phone book and we couldn't figure out how to remove it. Strange men kept buzzing her computer to try to get her to take phone calls. We had to permanently remove it from all of our PCs.

I was ready to give up on Internet phone services. Even if Skype fixed their poor-quality software, the hassles would still be there. I didn't like being tethered to the computer during phone calls (I normally welcome phone calls so I can get up and stretch). I also didn't like that I couldn't talk to anyone but other Skype users.

About six months later someone suggested I try Vonage for Internet phone calls. Vonage claimed that I could use real phones (instead of an uncomfortable computer headset) and that it worked like a phone, including allowing calls to anyone in the world, even non-Vonage users. Vonage's marketing made it clear that it wasn't going to be free (but it was inexpensive at $15/month), that it would work like a regular phone, with good voice quality, and that it required DSL (meaning it wouldn't work on the road).

Vonage had more restrictions and more costs; it would seem that Skype (free) had a better chance, yet it failed. I expected Vonage to bring similar disappointments. In fact, I was actually looking forward to watching Vonage fail so I could reaffirm my opinion that Internet phone calling was not consumer grade.

Instead, I was blown away. Vonage was great! They sent me a hardware box and told me how to hook it up to my DSL. The box was preprovisioned with my preassigned phone number from when I signed up, so it automatically configured itself. I then took my wireless house phone and plugged it into the back of the Vonage box. It worked!

The phone might as well be plugged into a wall. The sound quality is identical to a wall phone, and the phone itself is a regular phone, so I can use it wirelessly just as I did with my old wall phone. I can call anyone, including 911, and the price is exactly as advertised (inexpensive and with no extra charges). Vonage exceeded every expectation I could have had, including setup and provisioning.

Consumers have learned that "free" means either that strings are attached (like advertisements) or that the quality and usefulness will be very low. We don't mind paying for something—and you shouldn't be afraid of charging for something—if the value outweighs the costs.

Which takes us to "value": Most new products appear to be designed with a sense of equality between features. Good designers learn quickly what is important to their consumers and focus their limited resources on ensuring that the most important features are the easiest to get to and use.

Let's work together on this. Prioritize the following list:

A spam e-mail selling medication (solicitations)

A phone call from your spouse (personal)

A movie starring your favorite actor (entertainment)

A message from a coworker (your group)

A local weather forecast (generic information)

It is probably obvious how you rank this and, in fact, the way you rank it shows how you value different information (and how most consumers value information and features):

Highest value—Personal: Most people rank their spouse's phone call first, as it has direct personal value. The best products are those that solve direct personal problems.

High value—Entertainment: Next, you rank entertainment as high value. The more free time you have (and often the younger you are), the more value you get from entertainment.

Medium value—Your group: Your general friends (but not your close friends, which are more personal), your family (but not your closest family members), and your coworkers all fall a bit lower in value.

Low value—Generic information: Trying to sell generic information is the hardest, as there are too many ways for users to get this same information, and its commodity nature makes it cheap and easy for competitors to offer it as well. There will be market segments addicted to certain types of generic information (like people who are addicted to the weather), but the number of users willing to pay for it is usually small, and few need it urgently.

Negative value—Solicitations: You could call most solicitations negative value because they can cause users to stop using your product, and only 0.01% of users respond to them. Be careful how you use solicitations within your product or service.

If your product can provide strong personal value with low costs in terms of usability and the user's initial experience, then you are well on your way to Phase II adoption.

Improving the *Consumer Adoption Funnel*

We now have a complete *Consumer Adoption Funnel*:

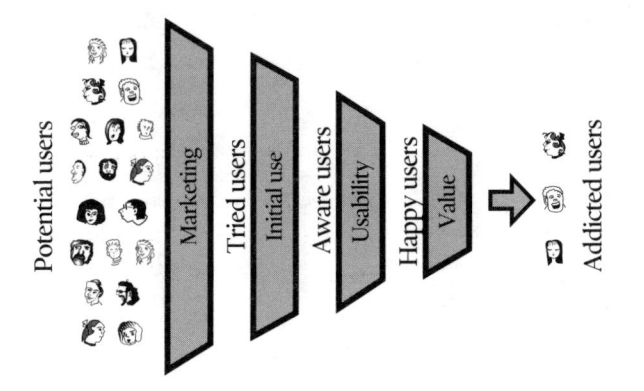

The natural instinct is to try to widen each gate so that more users pass through. This is exactly what you should do, but don't start doing this from left to right.

The different gates of the *Consumer Adoption Funnel* have different values to your company as you progress through the *Consumer Adoption S-Curve*. It turns out that the last gates in the funnel are most important in the early phases of the S-curve, whereas the first gate, marketing, is most important in Phase II and Phase III.

The S-curve below shows where the key funnel components have the most value:

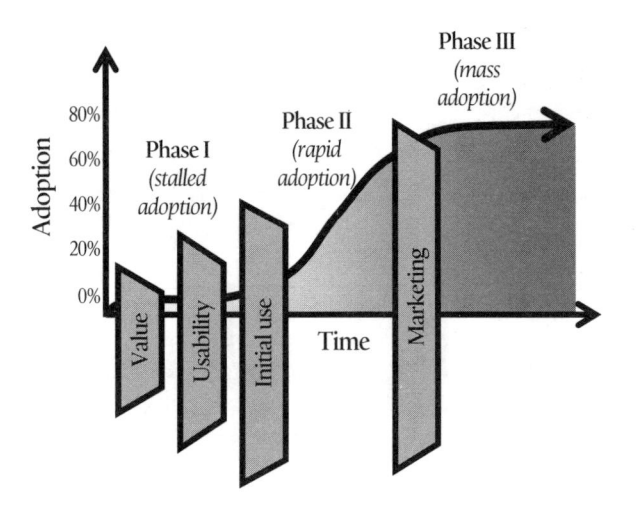

In this diagram, you see that your product's value must be well understood even before you launch the product. The problems your product solves should drive the initial design and deployment of the product.

Next, to transition into Phase II of the S-curve, your usability and initial use need to be optimized. This is how you develop a consumer-grade product.

Once your product is "sticky," i.e., can retain users with its good usability and value, you should focus on marketing to attract more users to trying your product.

In Phase III, your marketing changes slightly. You want to market the higher value, higher cost features that only addicted users will pay for. Increasing use of these features will increase your ARPU.

Conclusion: Success comes from the offering

Marketing and promotions alone don't determine product success. Marketing is only the first gate of four in the *Consumer Adoption Funnel*, and it can only cause users to try your product or service, not to become loyal users. Once you understand this, you can break through the myth that you need more marketing to be successful. Make sure your value is greater than your cost and consumers will increase their usage, ultimately leading to success.

You need to measure and optimize your *Consumer Adoption Funnel* gates to determine where and why users are not staying. Run usability tests and perform business intelligence analysis to find initial use faults and barriers and to determine where your users are really finding value. Monitor performance to make sure users are having quality experiences. Finally, once you have proven that your users are likely to become long-term repeat users, invest in the marketing and attraction programs that will entice more new users to try your offering—now that you know they will stay.

Myth 3:
If I'll use it, my users will

Reality:

*Consumers don't have your knowledge
or your motivation when they try
your product*

A common conversation in the offices of a consumer technology company:

Executive: "What features are you going to add in the next release?"

Product Manager: "Well, the engineers want the ability to customize the user interface, and we also ran a quick user test with the folks in sales and accounting and found that we need to add that new backup feature as well."

Executive: "Great. I didn't know we are testing with real users—that's great also. Can you also add a feature to..."

If you ever wondered why technology offerings have a maze of features that, in most cases, you never use or understand, then look no further. Most companies are not developing the product for you (even though they may think they are). They are developing it for themselves.

It begins when the company decides on features for a new release. The management, marketers, and engineers negotiate which features would be useful for their consumers. Naturally they immediately start asking around the office, "What features do you think we should add?"

Thus begins the creation of features for the company's employees, rather than for the consumer.

This practice fails—your employees are not your consumers. Employees know too much about their own products and services. They know how to use it, how to configure it, how to set it up, and how to get to its value. Consumers, on the other hand, have to endure each of these steps at full risk of failure.

Furthermore, employees don't pass through the *Consumer Adoption Funnel* with the same risks as consumers, nor do they evaluate the value versus cost seesaw presented in the last chapter. In most companies, the employees are *expected* to use their own products (i.e., they don't evaluate the *value* like a normal consumer). Also, employees usually don't pay to use the product or service, they can ask anyone around them for help, and often the product is set up or configured before the employee even starts using it (i.e., they don't have to evaluate the *cost* either). Although employees may be normal consumers in other markets, they are not normal consumers in their own market.

This chapter provides a better paradigm for viewing consumers that will help end this common misconception.

Three types of users

In terms of consumer behavior, there are basically three types of users who will use your product or service:

First-time users	Regular users	Power users
(every user is a first-time user when they first try your product)	*(users who like your product and use it on a regu- lar basis)*	*(users who work harder to find the value in your product)*

Each of these groupings of users has a different role in the success of your product, and they each behave differently. The best designers have a natural empathy to each of these groups of users, able to design products that will readily be accepted by each.

Everyone is a first-time user once

Every user of your product or service must begin with a first-time effort. Once your attraction and marketing programs have succeeded in convincing a user to give your product a try, your product goes through its first major test. Many things happen during a user's first experience, and understanding this experience through the eyes of your user, his state of mind, and his value to you and your product will drastically change how you deliver your product or service.

First, let's consider the value of first-time users. These users represent the first opportunity for creating long-term addicted users. The users who go on to successfully find the product's usability and value compelling will be your real user base. In other words, users who like what they see may go on to be regular users, while the users who decide not to use the product become lost opportunities:

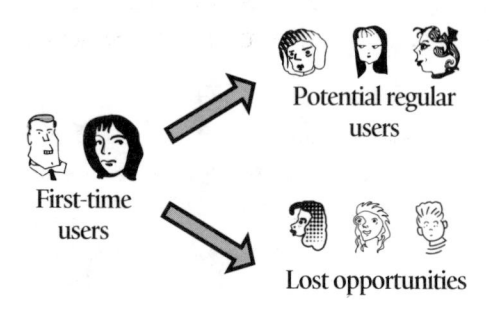

The value of first-time users is clear—they can become new regular users. The cost of ignoring them should also be clear, as the users who don't go on to become regular users may take years—and a lot of money—to get back.

You need to find a way to define, isolate, and measure the usage of your first-time users. I usually define *first-time user* as "any user who hasn't tried the product or service in the last six months." If someone hasn't used the product in six months, then they either have never tried the product or rejected the product the last time they used it. Now that they are trying it again, you have a renewed opportunity to capture them and keep them as regular users.

Once you have a clear definition of these users, you can tune your business intelligence engines to isolate these users for future analysis. In Internet environments this is done by looking at transaction logs to see which types of users are visiting the web site and what features (links) they are using.

Your users' state of mind matters

Now let's look at the first-time user's state of mind. To help you better understand each state of mind, I provide an example of how each state can be triggered by the ownership of an MP3 player:

> **Working mode:** In this mode, the consumer is trying to solve a real problem he cares about, like writing an e-mail or getting a stock quote. The user is typically doing something he has done many times and is more focused on the result or value of the task than on the mechanics of performing it.
>
> > To get an MP3 player to work, you need to find an online Internet store to buy the songs from, and you must select, pay for, and download those songs into the player. After doing this download process a few times, you find new download sessions put you into Working mode.
> >
> > You are in Working mode because you are focused on the goal of the task, not the details of executing the task. You already know where to go to get the music, you know how to pay for and download the music, and you know what to expect of the costs and quality of the music you download. All you think about during these download sessions is "What songs do I want?" and you spend very little thought on the actual details of performing the download process.
>
> **Entertained mode:** A consumer in Entertained mode is having fun, with no requirement or need to remember the activity in the long run (e.g., when watching TV, playing a game, or participating in a sport).
>
> > For MP3 players, this is listening to songs you have downloaded. If you hear a song you really like, you

may focus more on the details of the song like the words, background music, or the beat (you may even hum or sing along). If you hear a song that you don't like or are bored with, you may just skip to the next song, with no thought as to why. Your commitment to a particular song may be weak while in Entertained mode.

Buying-Learning mode: This is when someone is learning something that he wants to learn, such as how to use an MP3 player. Here the user finds it hard to question new ideas or interactively comment while he learns. Instead, he is busy listening, trying to keep up, trying to understand, and trying to remember.

This is a great state of mind because users are more willing to put up with barriers as they search for the solution to their problem.

When you first bought your MP3 player, you had a lot of hurdles to overcome. The purchasing process alone was likely confusing due to the many standards and capabilities, and, early on, also difficult due to the technical ways these players are sold. (Do I need a 256-megabyte player or will a 512-megabyte player do? How many songs does a megabyte even hold?)

Once the player is purchased, the downloading and digital rights issues provide new hurdles to overcome. Each hurdle during the purchasing and initial downloading process is committed to because you are in Buying-Learning mode, where you want to learn each step and your only goal is to successfully get to the next step. You put up with each new hurdle, even if it is frustrating, because you have a clear goal in mind that you are committed to (getting value out of your purchase).

Defensive-Learning mode: When users interactively challenge the information being fed to them, they are in Defensive-Learning mode. Ironically, people learn best when they are in Defensive-Learning mode (even if they don't agree with what they learned), because they must already have an opinion or context from which they interact with the "teacher." In this state of mind the user is looking for reasons to disagree or quit, causing small barriers to become magnified in his eyes. For example:

> If you found a web site offering "unlimited downloads of MP3 songs for $3.99 a month," you would probably approach it in Defensive-Learning mode. You would be skeptical that they would deliver on the promise and immediately start formulating ideas on how the site does this.

> If the web site is for a well-known brand, like Apple's iTunes or Wal-Mart, you might think they have a deal with certain recording labels, which allows them more freedom.

> If it isn't a well-known company, you would probably think that their selection of content is severely limited, or that they will go out of business before you get your money's worth (or that the songs won't be compatible with your player).

> Regardless, you will approach learning more from a defensive posture and will likely research deeper because you are looking for the "catch." But since you are defensive, you "jump ship" as soon as you find something that confirms your suspicions.

Being defensive is a natural means of self-preservation. Fortunately, it is also natural to reflect and to learn from your battles (whether you want to or not); thus Defensive-Learning mode is as much of a learning mode as it is a negative state of mind.

Curiosity-Learning mode: This is when someone is trying something new to see what it is like. The user is not committed to the new idea, process, or product but is curious enough to dedicate some time to trying it. Here is an opportunity to gain new users if your technology can provide some sort of entertainment. These users are likely to give up quickly, so the value must be obvious and compelling.

> To tie this to our MP3 player analogy, consider the parent of a child who has an MP3 player. Maybe you take your child to the dentist and your daughter leaves you with her MP3 player while you wait. You are bored, you have time to kill, and since you never really understood these things, you try to get it to work. You are in Curiosity-Learning mode.
>
> What happens next depends on the player (and possibly the music) that you have in your hands. You look for familiar mechanisms to turn it on and get it to play. You may even get it to play and spend time trying to turn down the volume (remember, this is your child), or skip to the next song (don't bother; you won't recognize any of them).
>
> Your commitment to this new technology is about as low as it gets. You didn't see yourself as a potential consumer for this product in the first place, and you are more likely than not looking for a way to quit more than a way to continue. At the first difficult step or bump in the experience, you will turn it off and go on to something else.

Curiosity-Learning mode can be a mixed blessing. On the one hand, this learning mode provides a great opportunity to capture new users. However, since these users are not committed to working through any problems with your product (they are only investigating during idle time), this is a tough mode for retaining users. This means that your chance of failure is at its highest. Don't expect many of these users to become addicted to your product unless you have a very simple consumer experience with very high value.

Clearly, there are other states of mind, but these are the most common ones that affect consumer behavior toward technology products.

State of mind affects behavior

Let's now consider how each state of mind affects consumer behavior. Users will resist, accept, or pursue different activities based on their state of mind. The nuances of your product and the users' states of mind will affect your users' decisions.

The table below rates key behaviors exhibited during the different modes of learning:

State of mind	Likeliness to *learn*	Willingness to *buy*	Willingness to *try*	Willingness to *stay*
Working	—			+
Entertained	—	+	+	+
Buying-Learning	+	+	+	+
Defensive-Learning	+			
Curiosity-Learning			—	—

Note: A minus sign "−" represents that consumers will resist the activity; no sign represents that consumers are ambivalent to the activity; and a plus sign "+" represents that consumers will likely pursue the activity.

Ignoring the needs or states of mind of first-time users in Phase I adoption will only delay your ability to grow into Phase II adoption. Never forget that every user starts as a first-time user, and only those who find simple value will go on to generate regular usage and revenue for your product.

Regular users are where the money is

Regular users behave completely different than first-time users. They like the product, they understand the product, and they use the product on a regular basis. As an added advantage, it is the regular user who drives the bulk of company revenues, making everyone happy.

Most companies become so infatuated with regular users that they spend all of their time only focusing on the needs of these users. This is easy to do because, as I said above, the designers have the most in common with these users. However, focusing on regular users to add more value may detract from the first-time user experience. As you will see later, too many features and options make the first-time user's experience even harder. Regular users don't have to worry about the barriers that got them to where they are (they are already there), whereas first-time users are still unaware of the product, its value, or how to get it to work for them.

The primary value of regular users is the revenue they generate. Secondary is that they can tell you, through their actions, where the real value in your product lies. Business intelligence analysis of regular users (especially analysis of the more addicted users in this group) can tell you which features are working so you can better position those features for first-time users.

The state of mind of a regular user is almost always one of the following (depending on the nature of your product):

Working mode, solving a problem: The user is using your product to solve a problem. Over time, the little steps required for each use become major frustrations. Regular users want to get to the value with as few steps as possible. Hence, I use Hotmail instead of Yahoo! e-mail, as Hotmail doesn't require me to retype my password every few days.

Entertained mode: The second most common state is that of being entertained. Here the user isn't trying to solve a problem, but is merely passing time. Again, these users don't want unnecessary steps or barriers between them and their entertainment.

It is important that you optimize your services to make them easier for regular users to get to the value quickly. If you are in Phase I or Phase II, your only goal for these users should be for them to become more addicted to the things they like, not to get them to pay more or use more things (don't put in new barriers). The side effect of optimizing your regularly used features is not only that regular users will find the value easier to get to, it also makes it easier for these high-value features to be discovered by first-time users.

Power users can make or break a product

I separate out power users even though they can also be considered first-time users and regular users as they progress with the product. The difference is that power users are more apt to search harder for your value and to use your product more often once the value is found.

Power users set the pace for the viral market success (or failure). They will typically be the first to try your product and the first to hype its value once they find it. Conversely, they will also be the first to openly criticize your product if they can't find any value or if it has too many barriers to usage.

This viral marketing (either good or bad) acts as an accelerant to your success or failure. It will either retard or lengthen your Phase I adoption or propel you into Phase II adoption and growth quickly.

> As an example of power users, think about the first time you used the Internet (assuming you can remember that experience). Was it influenced by other people or hype in newspapers and magazines, or did you decide on your own to try it on your PC?

> Most consumers were originally influenced in the 90s by a technically inclined friend or coworker. In fact, most people tried the Internet for the first time on another person's PC, as there were too many barriers to setting it up on their own computer first.

> Once you understood the value of the Internet, however, you were more willing to struggle through the barriers to setting it up on your own computer. These barriers to entry and low initial value (too few sites) kept the Internet out of reach from the mass market for years. Once power users started influencing everyone, and once the services started to appear, the value became clear and the adoption progressed rapidly. Power users helped spark the movement by spreading only good word of mouth to their friends. Very few power users were negative about the Internet, even when its value was unclear.

> Of course, the Internet has become a commodity nowadays, and when you buy a PC it is all set up and ready to go—this barrier has been removed.

Power users do not represent your entire market

Let's look at a bell curve of the entire potential market for a technology product, using the end user's technical skills as a means of differentiating the market:

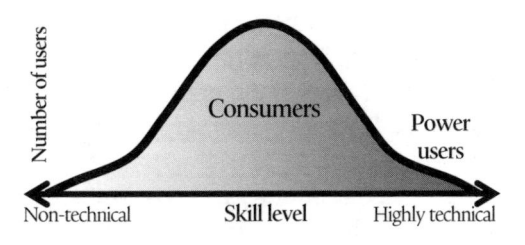

In this bell curve, "consumers" make up the bulk of the users (non-technical and all generally technical users), and "power users" are only at the far right tip of the bell curve.

Let me share an example of how power users appear when they show up in any of the hundreds of usability tests I've run in the past:

> In the average usability test, you may never see a power user. But one out of every 10–15 users will approach the product more methodically than the others.

> Inevitably, these methodical users identify themselves as power users, usually claiming to be the "go to" person for technological issues among friends and coworkers. They learned quickly how to solve problems better than others and enjoy their role as the expert among their peers.

> Their scientific approach to solving problems was obviously different from the rest of the users: They tried every feature in a logical pattern and showed an uncanny ability to remember the navigational paths they took so that they could backtrack and re-traverse different paths.

This style of usage allowed them to embrace the product quicker and usually meant quick success at solving the tasks thrown at them in the usability testing setting. Their behavior is proactive and patient—they know that in real life they don't have someone else to turn to for help.

Lately I have had the opportunity to analyze business intelligence data to help identify and watch the real behavior of power users (as well as to count them). Only 4–6% of the population exhibited power user characteristics. Below is a list of the most common tendencies of power user:

Power users are a small market: Power users never make up a large part of a market. Most markets (even in Japan) have fewer than 8% of these users. Don't overestimate this number.

Power users are proactive: This is the most defining difference between power users and average consumers. Power users approach products proactively, looking at barriers as challenges to be solved, not as reasons to quit.

Power users are critical: Power users are very critical of the products they use. They understand that they can't recommend a product that has poor usability and are quick to point out stupid barriers as they use products.

Power users are vocal: They will tell their friends what to use and what to avoid. They expect their friends to consult them, so they try to learn about new technology in advance of these questions.

Power users will customize: Power users are not intimidated by products with lots of options—in fact, they will look for ways to customize services. Don't misread this attribute, however. Power users customize to achieve efficiency but will criticize the initial product for requiring customization. They will always prefer a more usable base product.

You should provide customization options for these users (they do want them), but don't use the fact that these options exist as an excuse for poor usability (see "Don't make it a setting," later).

Power users are looking for a way to say "Yes": When power users first use your product, they will look hard to find a way to get the product to work properly. Power users seem to have a built-in desire to find a product's value. Only when they are forced to stumble through too many barriers or when they find too little end value will they reject a product.

Now let's look at the non-Power users, which I simply call "consumers." Analysis through usability tests and business intelligence has shown the following traits:

Consumers are a large market: These users represent the true market opportunity for a product, and in general should be the key focus when designing technology products. Usually if you can satisfy a consumer, you will satisfy most power users.

Consumers are reactive: Unlike power users, consumers will not make extra effort to find value in a product. They react to what they see and will not customize or search for efficiency or value.

Consumers are quiet: Consumers will quietly try and fail with your product. They won't send you letters or complaints; they will just stop using the product. They are not as judgmental as power users; they just "take it or leave it."

Consumers will not customize: Whenever I use business intelligence to analyze customization features of consumer products, I inevitably find that less than 8% of users even use these features (the power users). Forcing a consumer through a customization option is not a solution—it is a guarantee that few users will use your product.

Consumers are looking for a way to say "No": Consumers don't have the patience, drive, or the mentality to work through problems or barriers in order to get to the value of your product. Huge numbers of users will stop using with each additional step you introduce between them and success.

Notice a common theme here? Consumers are direct opposites of power users. Look at the contrast in this table:

Power user	Consumer
Small market (3–8%)	Large market (85–95%)
Proactive	Reactive
Critical/vocal	Passive/quiet
Will customize	Won't customize
Want to say "Yes"	Want to say "No"

Don't make it a setting...

Making design choices into settings almost became a major myth in this book. The problem is that many designers argue about features, which is natural, and at some point the conflicts regarding how a feature should work are settled by making the choice a preference or setting "so the user can decide."

This is a myth. Users don't decide. In fact, other than a few power users, most consumers will never change your settings. This is hardest for engineers to believe, because, unlike consumers, engineers do change their settings. But aren't engineers power users by definition?

The reality in product design is that whatever you set as the default preferences will be the permanent settings for 95% of your market. Don't fall victim to thinking your users will customize your service to work for them. Find a way to personalize your service automatically to meet the users' needs reactively. The reasons are well defined above. Only power users are proactive enough to change preferences. I have seen this in every consumer market I've worked in.

A better way to solve these feature conflicts is to first try to think like a true consumer. Adding the preference is okay, since some power users may like that preference, but make sure the default behavior for that preference is the most productive and natural method for the bulk of your users. Only the power users will ever need to change the preference to a mode that works better for them.

Usually, the best personalization features happen automatically in reaction to the user's past behavior and decisions—they do not require any proactive customization by the user. These reactive personalizations are harder to conceive and are usually harder to implement, but they are more powerful for consumers.

> A great example of a proactive versus a reactive feature is the spell checker in Microsoft Word. Originally, the spell checker required a proactive step of running the spell checker on the document and fixing the errors one by one. This feature was seldom used and its benefit to the product was not being maximized.

Microsoft changed the way this feature worked so that it now automatically spell-checks the documents in the background and interactively places a red squiggly line under misspelled words. This immediate feedback during the typing process provides a reactive way of handling spelling errors that is infinitely more useful to consumers.

Even better, later versions of Word started automatically correcting simple or obvious misspellings as they are typed. For example, while I was typing the word "simple" earlier in this paragraph I accidentally hit the keys out of order and typed "ismple." Not to worry—Word autocorrected it. This is the best possible user experience, where the user doesn't have to perform any actions to get the correct behavior from the product.

Features like this are also greatly appreciated by power users. This eliminates the need for them to run separate spell checking programs as well.

In its old state, the spell check feature in Word was occasionally used by a few users. Today, as a reactive "solution," 99% of users access the spell checker every time they use the product. This represents universal success in terms of consumer feature design.

Let's consider another example:

Microsoft's Internet Explorer is also reactive because it "remembers" input field information. This saves time by automatically completing the fields as the user types.

This time-saving convenience doesn't require any proactive steps by the user—it's just there, and it works. Users don't have to constantly retype common phrases like their user name every time they use the browser.

This feature not only saves effort, but it fixes poor usability design of the web sites the user visits. Since these sites don't "remember" this information, Microsoft solved the problem by making it a feature of the browser. Best of all, they solved it in a way that is reactive for the consumer, not requiring proactive steps.

Although reactive personalization is usually better, sometimes it can be disorienting to users:

> Another feature in recent releases of Microsoft Word that frustrates some users is that it hides options that have not recently been used within its menus. Actually, the whole Windows operating system currently performs this way.

> This is a reactive feature in that it automatically occurs without the user proactively turning it on, but it is also a mistake from a consumer usage perspective.

> If a user knows that a feature is available and can't find it (say they've used it before, but the software has helpfully "hidden" it since it was a long time ago), they will be frustrated. Consumers (and power users, for that matter) need consistency of approach. If they can't find something, the learning process takes longer. If the learning process takes longer, the addiction process takes longer.

> Ah, but of course, the engineers tell us, you can turn that particular option off. It's a setting…

> In this case, the setting (which very few consumers will find and change) is set to the wrong default. Let power users turn it on—don't make consumers turn it off (they won't).

Build loyalty through reactive customization

Another great way to retain users is to use their first-time user experiences to create loyalty. Instead of providing an inflexible first-time experience (e.g., asking many up-front questions before providing access to the feature or product), use the introductory session to learn about the user passively by observing the users' actions as they explore the product or feature. Then, when a user repeats a task, use this early knowledge to provide answers quicker or deliver features the way the user has shown a preference for. Use the users' past behaviors to dynamically change the product to one that will behave better with each use and you will also create loyalty to your product.

Ali provided a few good examples of how a business won his loyalty by customizing its products and services for him in a re-active manner:

> Ali is very tall (6' 5"). If he buys regular shirts from a typical store, he ends up with his shirt hanging out of his pants, so he buys shirts that are a bit longer than normal. He also has very long arms, so he buys shirts from a specialized shirt maker in London who knows his sizes and delivers the shirts by mail.

> One time when the package arrived, an insert was included that let customers know they could order on the web site. Technology meets custom-made shirt retailing. Although Ali has had bad past experiences ordering custom products on the Internet (the results never match the desired experience), this turned out to be a good experience.

> In this case, there was no need for registration to view the range of shirts, it was easy to identify what was available, and it was easy to place the order. Ali still had to fill out forms to make the order, but that's to be expected.

> Better still, when the confirmation e-mail arrived, it mentioned that all the sizing information would be retained. There would be no need to reenter these preferences the next time he visits the site. And, during clearance time, those items available in his size are presented first.

What did your favorite company do with their product or service to remember you or to gain your loyalty? Can you measure it against the costs? Are they using technology to improve their services? Find a way to proactively capture your customers' behaviors and desires, and the increase in adoption and regular usage will pay for itself.

Conclusion: You do not represent your users

You have vast knowledge of your offering. You know how to set it up, navigate in it, where the best features are, and how to get to that value, and you already respect that value. You may not be a power user in other markets, but you are a power user in your own market; because of this, you overlook all of the barriers that the average consumer sees when they use the product.

Don't design and market for yourself—you are trying to say "Yes." Instead, observe how consumers find ways to say "No." Look for unnecessary complexities and customization requirements, or long installation processes that are probably killing your product's success.

Finally, don't add settings or preferences to your product as a way to solve design disputes today. Design your product correctly instead. Spend the extra time to understand consumer behavior and you will be rewarded by usage.

Myth 4:

Consumers will find a product's value

Reality:

The value must find the user

Does your product or service have many features or options? Do you try to organize your product so that users can sift through the features to find the ones that have the most value for them? If you do, then you're likely jeopardizing your product's success. The reality is that users won't search very far for value.

You must quickly get users to your product's key value.

Analyzing user types

In the last six years of consumer behavior consulting, Ali and I had an opportunity few consumer experts ever get: We were able to help design a business intelligence system that analyzed user behavior at a deeper level than simply counting raw transactions (we did this for the mobile phone market). In this chapter we will show how we used this technology to answer a basic question we had from the beginning of time: "How many users do you lose per key-click?" (Or, in other words, how does the layout of your product and features affect a user's decision to explore or use those features?)

Before answering these questions, we must first explain the basic methodology we used so you understand how to duplicate this analysis for your products and services.

First, you will need data. Most businesses have access to user transactions, such as Internet web site transactions or retail purchasing information. However, even without direct business intelligence, you can poll your users to see how they use your product, which is something I had to depend on in my early career. User registration can also tell you which features prompted the purchase and which features were used on a regular basis (although capturing real information is always more complete and telling than what is gathered from the somewhat self-selecting group who fill in registration screens and answer queries).

No matter how you measure your users' activities, you should separate out the fundamental categories of users, as mentioned in the last chapter. For analysis purposes, you should split your users into the following subcategories to get a clear view of the usage of your products:

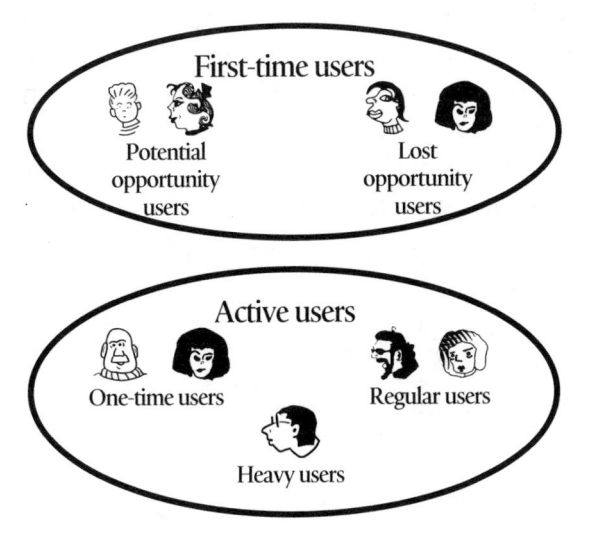

This breakup only makes sense if you look at a fixed period of time, because all users were first-time users at one time, and most users will have visited your service more than once over a long period of time. After many iterations and experiments, we have found that the best analysis is done by looking at only one week's worth of data. In other words, if you can isolate all of the activity for your product for a period of one week, you will have enough information to optimize your product or service to increase adoption.*

Once you pull the data, try to separate the transactions that are caused by each of the following user categories:

---

*In our studies we found that adding extra weeks to the analysis made less than a 1% difference over a large base of consumers. However, we did find a few examples where one week wasn't representative of typical usage, and you will need to determine what is best for your product category (especially if your product doesn't draw much usage in a typical week). In most cases you can use a week's data, but be careful which week you select; you will need to account for differences such as seasonal (e.g., Christmas versus summer), events (e.g., during the World Cup), promotional periods (e.g., a free trial period), and change of services (e.g., a web site introducing a new feature).

First-time users: These are all the users who tried your product during the week in question, either for the first time or for the first time in the last six months.

There are two important subsets of first-time users:

Potential opportunity users: These are first-time users who came back within three days of their first use. They are showing signs of potentially becoming regular users, so their first experiences provide you with an opportunity to find out what caused them to return (i.e., what value did they find that others didn't find on their first visit?).

Lost opportunity users: These are first-time users who didn't return in the first three days after their first visit. These examples of failures tell you how a poor early experience affects your users' perspective.

Active users: These are any users, other than first-time users, who used your product during the week being analyzed. We break these users into three subcategories:

One-time users: These users only used your product or service once during the entire week being analyzed. These users act similar to a first-time user in that they don't use the product much, quitting when the value is not found quickly and easily.

Regular users: These users returned to your product two to nine times during the week being analyzed (you may use your own metrics to separate Regular from Heavy users, but be consistent). Since they are using the product on a regular basis, they have found some value that is driving their return.

Heavy users: These users returned to your product ten or more times during the week being analyzed. The heavy user category differs from the regular user category mostly because it contains your power users and addicted users, and the services they use are predictive of where your product's value is.

During a one-week analysis we want to look for answers to two questions: "Where are the users going?" and "Where should the users go?" (i.e., where is the value?). Answering both questions will help predict what happens if you change the approach to your product's presentation of its value.

Where do we want users to go?

The best example to demonstrate that users won't "hunt" for value comes from the European mobile Internet market we discussed earlier. In Europe, users were presented with menus that allowed them to find the services they wanted to use (this is very similar to most products and how they present their features to the user, so you can apply it to your product as well). This has proven to be a major failure in terms of consumer adoption, so we did business intelligence analysis on many service offerings for most of the major European mobile phone operators to determine what was failing.

Consider the following example of a set of mobile Internet service menus (I've used dotted lines to show that many of the other services have hierarchal submenus that are not displayed here):

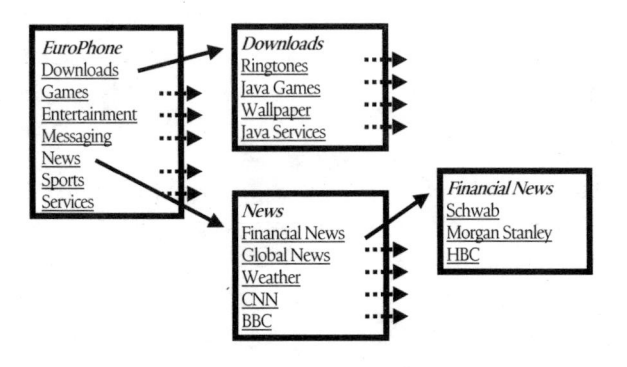

This menu structure is designed to meet a logical progression. Here, the goal is to ensure that each service can be found by navigating the menus using categories that go from the general to the specific. Obviously, this structure can be quite deep, allowing any service to be found by navigating the menus.

Operators use this logical design to meet two basic objectives: (1) There is a service for every user and (2) users will find the service they like most.

This design is flawed. It assumes a consumer behavior that, at the time, wasn't proven. Displaying all available features or navigational paths to all users is a common mistake among products with poor consumer adoption. The designers violate many principles pointed out in this book, including: Trying to reach too broad a market segment (a service for every user), expecting users to search for value (consumers won't look far), and assuming that consumers can handle the navigational task (too many steps and too many decisions create too many opportunities for consumers to say "No").

Split up your user data...

So how do we prove that the European navigational method works or fails? First, look at the transaction data to determine where the different types of users go. The data we collected while looking at different major phone operators helps to clarify which users fall into which categories and tells us where users go within the portals.

The data presented here will be aggregated to help protect the individual operators' identities and internal data. But by aggregating many operators who were in Phase I consumer adoption during our analysis, we were able to see clear trends in usage (and, in fact, operator-to-operator results varied by only 1–3% from each other).

Operators find many surprises when we present the analysis of their services. The first surprise usually is the number of users that fell into each of the top categories of users. What do you think the split of users is for your product? How many heavy users or first-time users would you expect in any given week?

The Europeans had a very large number of users (92%) who either never tried the service, or, if they did, were dormant during the week analyzed. In fact, on average, only 8% of customers used the service during the week we analyzed (in 2004):

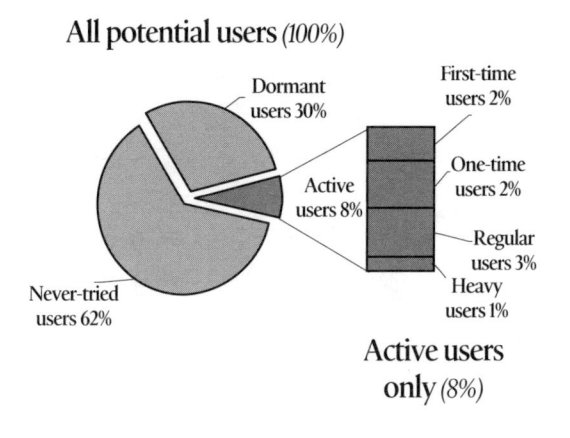

All potential users *(100%)*

Dormant users 30%

First-time users 2%

Active users 8%

One-time users 2%

Regular users 3%

Heavy users 1%

Never-tried users 62%

Active users only *(8%)*

Consider the information in the pie chart above compared to the *Consumer Adoption Funnel* (pictured again here):

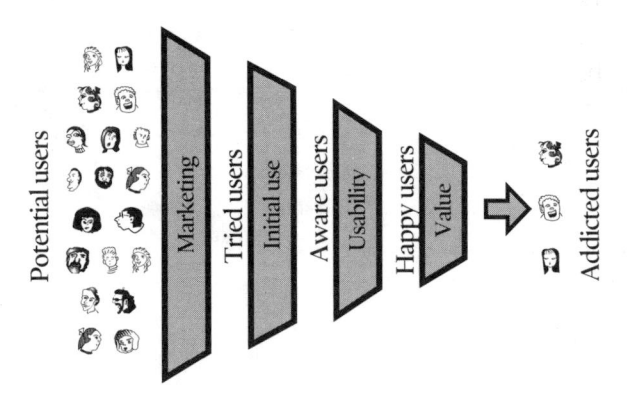

The potential users of the funnel are all users counted in the pie chart, including never-tried users, dormant users, and active users. The tried users in the funnel are the two slices of the pie holding dormant and active users. The addicted users in the funnel are only the subset of the active users' slice of the pie that include regular users and heavy users (which sum up to be only 4% of the total potential users).

Next, we will focus only on the 8% of users who were active and look at them in a 3-dimensional pie chart:

Active users *(8% of all potential users)*

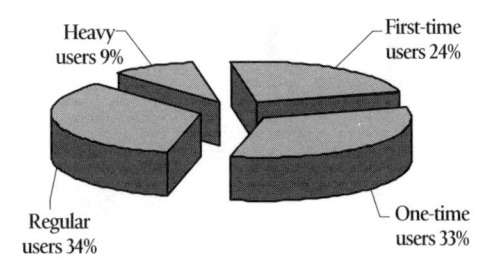

The left-hand slices of the pie (heavy users and regular users) as those users who have already chosen to use the service (i.e., repeat users). The right-hand slices (first-time users and one-time users) are hopeful future opportunities for repeat use. More than half (57%) of the users were not regular or heavy users, meaning that there were many more opportunities to create future repeat users, but very little adoption was happening so far.

Compare this to the usage for each type of user, which is done by looking at the total number of minutes each category of users spent using the services:

Minutes of usage generated by active users

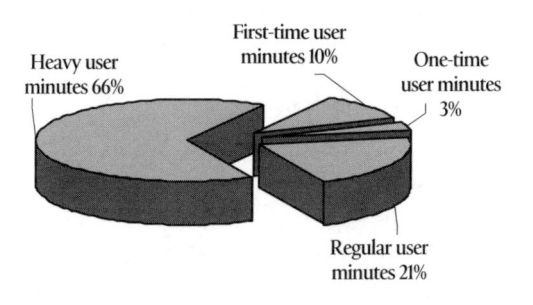

First-time user minutes 10%

One-time user minutes 3%

Heavy user minutes 66%

Regular user minutes 21%

The heavy users and regular users dominate the usage of the service (collectively, 87% of the minutes are generated by these repeat users). This demonstrates the value of addicted users and shows how little first-time users and one-time users contribute (which may also explain why so many companies ignore them). However, since only 8% of the total potential user base was active (remember, these 3-dimensional pie charts are only for the 8% of *active users* and exclude the other 92% of never-tried and dormant users), it may be wiser to focus on converting more first-time users and one-time users into regular and heavy users.

In summary, the last three pie charts prove that heavy and regular users will generate the bulk of the usage (which most companies convert into revenue). However, since usage only matters when generated by many users, your focus during Phase I and Phase II of the S-curve should be on converting first-time users and one-time users into regular and heavy users.

Stickiness versus attraction

Now that we have the users divided up, let's extrapolate the data to see what happens if we look at "stickiness" versus "attraction." In Myth 2 we said that attraction programs weren't always the right next step in Phase I of the *Consumer Adoption S-Curve*. Now that we have some real data, let's extrapolate the data over several months and see if this is true.

First, consider the pie charts of the last section. Here we showed that, on average, about half (57%) of the active users were first-time users and one-time users; i.e., users who are not yet repeat users. This means that during this sample week only half (43%) of the active users could be considered to have truly adopted the product.

To put into real numbers, let's pretend that an operator has a potential user base of 10 million users. Since there are only 8% active users, this would mean only 800,000 users visit the service during an average week. Of that, using roughly rounded numbers, 200,000 are first-time users and 200,000 are one-time users, meaning there are 400,000 potential candidates for new long-term customers in a given week (the other 400,000 are already converted into regular and heavy users). Furthermore, if you extrapolate from one week to one month, you can expect around four times as many first-time users (4 × 200,000 = 800,000), and twice as many one-time users since many visit only once every two weeks ($2 \times 200,000 = 400,000$), or 1.2 million first- and one-time users.

Thus, in any particular month this operator has 1.2 million new opportunities to create long-term users (from its first- and one-time users), whereas there are only about 400,000 existing long-term users (from its regular and heavy users). If we run this chart out over time, the repeat user base (or adoption) looks like this:

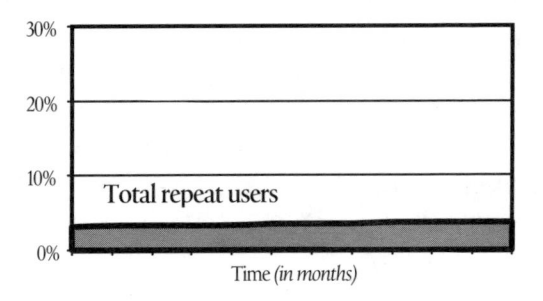

As you can see, there is about 1% of adoption growth over the given time period, which in this case is one year. This is exactly what a stalled Phase I adoption curve looks like, as there is no sustainable growth spike.

Now consider what happens if this operator performs a major marketing campaign with price discounts over a few months.

We've analyzed a few customers in this phase, and what we see is the following type of adoption curve before, during, and after the marketing campaign:

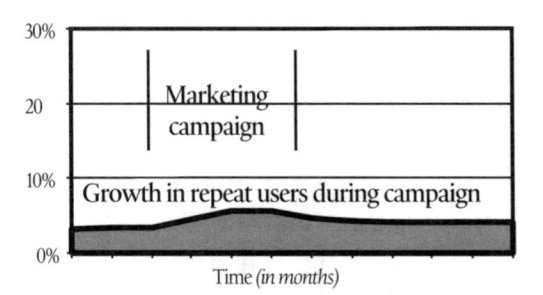

Notice how the marketing campaign caused what appeared to be adoption growth, but after the campaign ended there is a fall-off again, and the operator goes back into a growth phase like before, with slow-growing adoption. This is very common in Phase I adoption, and it is sad to watch people spend so much money to attract users only to find that their overall growth hasn't really changed.

With our business intelligence data we can now explain why this happens. Let's overlay the new users trying the service each month on the original adoption curve:

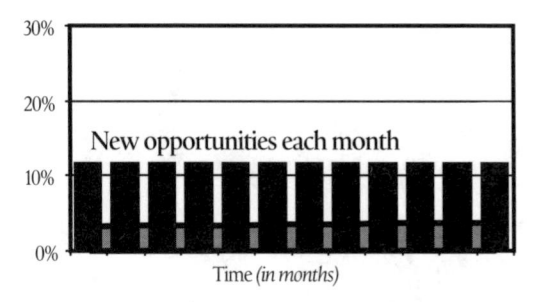

Here's a common trick most marketers use in their external communications: They report the total number of users visiting each month, including the non-repeating users shown in the black bars above, as their total adoption—thus making it look like they have 11–15% adoption, when in fact they are between 3 and 4% adoption. Although this may be a normal external practice, be careful not to start believing your own marketing hype. Break out the numbers and treat it realistically internally if you really want adoption.

What is the first thing that jumps out at you when you look at the black bars above the gray adoption curve in the last chart? You can see that there is a serious stickiness problem and no need for marketing or attraction programs (after all, about 10% of the potential user base tries the service each month already). How could so many new users try a product each month and not cause a faster growth in adoption?

The answer can be found in the next chart, which overlays the number of users who don't become regular users each month (in other words, this is the churn for the product—they tried it, but didn't like it):

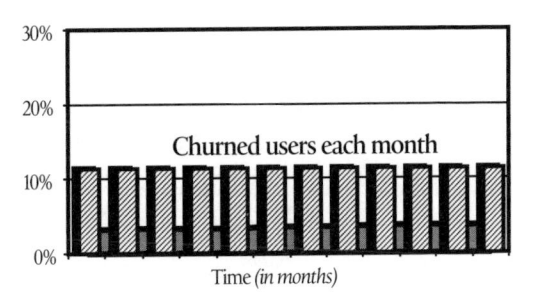

Here you see that slightly fewer users (in striped bars) are giving up on the product each month out of those who try it (in black bars behind the striped bars).

Thus, adoption can be measured as the difference between
those who try a product and those who give up on it. Raising
the attraction (those who try it) by marketing the product
more will automatically cause an equal rise in the churn. This
isn't increasing adoption (as we said in Myth 1).

What happens if you focus on the product's stickiness to keep
more users from giving up on the product?

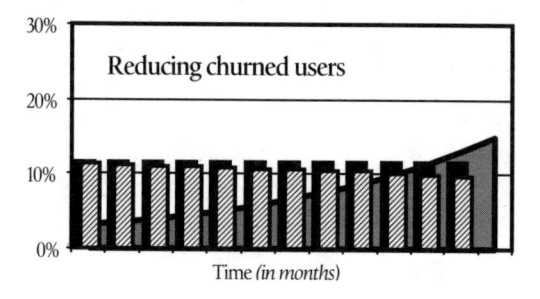

Notice the bigger gaps between those who try the product
(black bars) and those who churn from the product (striped
bars). Now the adoption area begins showing true adoption by
entering into Phase II of the *Consumer Adoption S-Curve*. Con-
gratulations!

Stop churning users

The reason most users churn from products is that they never
find the product's value. Usually this is because the value is
hidden from the users and the product is designed under the
assumption that users will search for that value. Our data
proves that users will not behave this way.

Let's go back to looking at the mobile Internet portal presented earlier (you can do the same thing with your own product, but instead of portal sites as shown here, list the navigational hierarchy for your features):

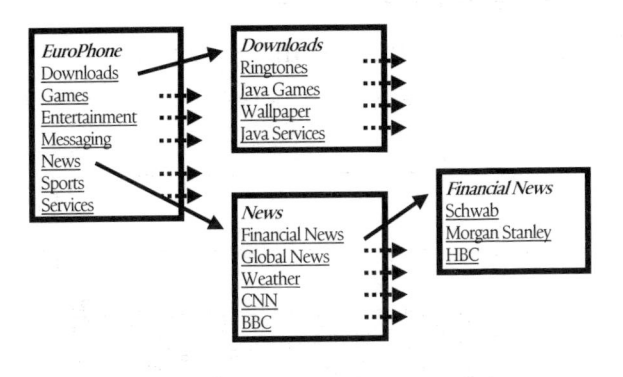

Now let me ask you, if you know that you have 200,000 new first-time users, where do you think they go? Most designers assume there would be equal distribution throughout the portal due to users finding the services that fit their needs best. Reality, however, can now be measured.

In our analysis of major mobile phone operators with Phase I services like the example above, we found a very consistent flow for users through the menus of features and subservices. In particular, we were able to determine and predict exactly how many users would try each option in each menu simply due to its position. So I ask you again: If 200,000 new users tried the portal, how many of those tried the 5th option (News) on the first page?

Our models can accurately predict that only 13% of new users who enter any page on a mobile Internet menu will try the 5th option. Thus, if 200,000 users visited the portal, on average around 26,000 users will try this item. It gets worse as you go down the portal. Only 2.3%, or 4,600 users out of a total available audience of 200,000, will try the 11th item.

In fact, the model predicts broadly that about 50% of users will continue down to any follow-on menu item as they scroll from the top item to the bottom (i.e., the cost of a key-click is a loss of half of your customers).

For any particular portal (or software product or Internet site), you can analyze and predict the expected number of users who will visit each item (or feature or link). In our example, I've rolled up the global averages of 8 major operators' portals in Phase I consumer adoption:

Item position	Expected users
1st item	33.5%
2nd item	19.3%
3rd item	14.3%
4th item	14.0%
5th item	13.2%
6th item	10.4%
7th item	7.5%

In other words, irregardless of the item that appears on a menu, the usage was found to be influenced more by its position than its content or label (remember, this is a based on a constrained device, the mobile phone). This proves that users "give up" the more they have to click (as we showed in an earlier chapter regarding the use of Chat).

Using these global numbers, we can now calculate what we might expect from our example portal for each menu item for 200,000 new users:

Item position	Our example menu	Expected users
1st item	Downloads	67,000
2nd item	Games	38,600
3rd item	Entertainment	28,600
4th item	Messaging	28,000
5th item	News	26,400
6th item	Sports	20,800
7th item	Services	15,000

Furthermore, if a user clicks to select a menu item, like News, we found through separate analysis that only 65% of those users will continue to use the submenu that appears (many will either not wait for the screen, or look at the page, select nothing, and either go back or quit). By the time you are in the HBC menu (3 menu levels down), there will only be 347 first-time users left.[†] Of these 347 users, none have found value yet, as they now have to navigate the HBC menus to get to its value (a news page or stock quote).

The above example showed that of 200,000 users, only 347 would find the application HBC. However, this assumes that

---

[†]For those of you who can't believe this, here's the math: $200,000 \times .132 \times .65 \times .335 \times .65 \times .143 \times .65 = 347.31$. Here's the logic: 200,000 users come to the service, 13.2 % select the 5th item, *News*, of which only 65% will continue (the other 35% will likely quit while waiting for *News* to load, or quit immediately after seeing the *News* menu and recognizing that it isn't what they want). Of the 17,160 users who selected the *News* menu, 33.5% will select the first link, *Financial News*, and 65% of those will continue in the *Financial News* menu once it appears, leaving only 3,737 users; 14.3% of these will select the third link in *Financial News* to take them to HBC, and only 65% will continue from there. This leaves only 347 users.

each user will make a perfect navigation path to the application that they want.

In reality, users will look for something they want and not navigate perfectly. Consider, for example, a user looking for sports news. In usability tests we find that users don't look at an entire menu and then select Sports. Instead, they navigate down one item at a time, evaluate that item, and then make a decision to select it or not.

For example, if they see an item that says Entertainment, they will try it for sports (and will fail), then they will try News (and it will also fail), and then they will go down the Sports path.

Because of business intelligence analysis, we know that users spend less than 2 minutes on their first visit before giving up. In the usability test they can easily take 20–30 minutes to find Sports and get an update. As an observer, we know that these users are being stretched beyond their reasonable limits as a consumer.

By confirming the usability test results with the business intelligence results, we can now prove definitively that the navigation model is broken and will not work with real consumers behaving normally. It must be fixed.

Since the tables provided in this section are averaged across many menus for menu operators, the averages are somewhat generic. When you apply real items like Downloads versus Travel to menus, you will see larger or smaller user counts for that item than expected. This difference tells us which services overperform compared to the averages and which underperform. This normalization, when done right, can be done against attraction, stickiness, and usage (minutes of use) as well.

By identifying the features that overperform and optimizing access to them, and by removing or burying the underperform-ers, a company can improve the overall stickiness of their services or products for first-time users. This optimization decreases the number of failed first-time user experiences, reduces churn, creates more regular and heavy users, and starts Phase II adoption.

Conclusion: Your value must find your users

All of this data proves one major thing: You must determine what your value is for your product or service and make sure it is prominently positioned so that users will find and use it early. Every key-click, mouse-click, or navigational decision presents another opportunity for consumers to say "No." We know that consumers are reactive and will not make proactive searches for value (like power users). Hiding your value will ruin your consumer adoption.

In our analysis of many major services, the average first-time user will only spend 1.7 minutes trying the service before giving up. Don't hope your users will find that valuable feature on their own—you get precious little time with them. If they make one navigational mistake or find one poor service or feature, they will not return.

Myth 5:

Consumers want more features

Reality:

Consumers only want a few key features, and they want them to work well

As an idea turns into a product and starts shipping, its designers and engineers seem to have an unlimited number of new ideas for new features to include in the next version, each feature designed to make the product "more complete" in the designer's eyes. However, in the eyes of the consumer, the exact opposite is happening. The early users are wondering why the key feature is so hard to use, buggy, or incomplete. Consumers don't want more features muddying up the value, they want the key features to work well.

When fixing a new product that is in stalled adoption, it may feel like all you have is your professional training to aid in your decisions. Engineers try to engineer their way to success by adding features (often power user features); marketing people tinker on the marketing (the surgeon wants to operate, the doctor wants to medicate).

However, since your product is now shipping, you have more than your training and experience to drive decisions: You now have users. You can now build a record of their behavior using your product. It is now time to let the data tell you what your next step should be.

Not only are the designers of the product in "guess mode" for version 1, most are also power users (designers know too much). When they move on to design version 2, they continue this behavior of guessing and design for themselves (see Myth 3). This means that designers stay in guess mode and more features are added to make the product better for the power users—not for new consumers.

Even worse, sometimes management dictates that new features should be added to make the product appeal to a broader audience, in the hope of attracting new market segments to the product. By targeting all consumers, the new product has no specific user targeted for its improvement (and no users will want or use the product).

In the previous chapter, we showed that users won't search for value, and by adding new features the company is increasing the forest of features the consumer has to search through to find the true value of the product. Many companies don't even know where their product's true value is. This chapter shows why too many features hurt adoption, how to find the value of your product, and how to focus your energy more productively on cleaning up the portion of the product that accelerates consumer adoption growth.

Where is the value?

If users will not search for value in a product, then the designers have to: (1) Find the value in the product and (2) ensure that your product is designed so that new users will also find that value when they first try the product.

The better your understanding of how consumers use your products, the better your decisions for future features and enhancements will be. You should have a very clear idea of how your current features perform, as well as what problem these features solve for your users. In the last chapter, we showed how little effort a first-time user will give to your product. Now let's look at the adopted users (the regular and heavy users) to determine where your value is.

Regular users and heavy users keep returning to your product to access the key features that are valuable to them. Many of these early users were probably power users with problems they needed solved—otherwise, they wouldn't have spent as much time finding your value and staying with your product through its early stages. Furthermore, these repeat users continue to live every day with the inefficiencies of your product (or they found a way to customize your product to make it easier to access their favorite features).

Optimizing your product to make the high-value features easier to access has two direct benefits: (1) It makes it less likely that current adopted users will tire of the effort to access these features and (2) it helps first-time users and one-time users find these features and potentially become addicted as well. There is no downside here.

To find the value you only have to look at the usage of the regular users and heavy users, with emphasis on analyzing the heavy users, because they are clearly the most addicted.

To analyze repeat users, you need to first isolate their usage statistics from the first-time users and one-time users. The transactions of wandering first-time users will throw off your data—remove it. The occasional use of one-time users is also not very important, as it shows potential dead ends in your product—remove them also. With the isolated data of only regular users and heavy users, you are now prepared to see what is important.

Next, you need to find a way to analyze the data that allows the different features to be compared equally to each other (apples-to-apples, as they say). The biggest violator of apples to apples comparisons in the Internet world today is the individual web "hit" or "transaction" recorded in a web log. Don't fall into the trap of counting raw transaction data (if you are analyzing a web site). Transactions can often be misread because users of two different features may generate unrealistically different transaction volumes:

> For example, a web site that provides games will likely load in a lot of graphics and require many transactions as the user plays the game. Most web servers treat each individual graphic as a separate transaction with a unique URL. Thus, loading a single page will take 10–20 transactions (1 click for the user, but many transactions to load the page).

> Another web page showing an e-mail message may only generate 1 page of text, which is logged as only 1 transaction on the web server.

> If you are looking at transactions, you will think that the game is 10–20 times more important than the e-mail message since the game created 10–20 transactions. Yet the e-mail may be more valuable to the user and cause more stickiness (return visits).

> Your job is to normalize these different services so you can accurately compare their performance using valid metrics.

I recommend that you look at other attributes of each feature, not just their transaction volume. Below are key metrics that will help determine a feature's real value:

Usage (minutes of use): How long does a user spend on a feature? This is a good clue to the feature's value to the user (especially if the product is a service that has a price or charge for minutes of use). Often this can be pulled out and estimated from transaction data by looking at the time stamps on each transaction. Minutes of use is a measure of usage (often related to revenue), however, and doesn't imply stickiness. Aggregate this data into an "average usage per user" (or average minutes per user) to get the best benchmark on the average usage.

Stickiness (return visits): If users return to one feature more often than others, that feature has a high stickiness. Stickiness is perhaps the best indicator of a feature's true value with its users, as a feature that has few users returning to it isn't working, while one that has many users returning often must be delivering value.

Attraction (unique users): This is the count of users who visit a particular feature (called "unique users" because each user is only counted once, even if they return to the feature many times). Although this is an important metric, there are two areas where you have to be careful when using this metric. First, if a feature is buried, it will naturally have fewer visits than one that is more highly placed (as was shown in the last chapter). You need to find a way to normalize attraction based on the number of steps to get to the feature. Second, attraction measures perceived value, not real value. A feature that is very easy to try or a feature that appears to offer something that it doesn't actually deliver may have high attraction but very low usage and stickiness.

Feature categories: Sometimes it is easier to group features into categories so you can see relative differences between categories. An example of this would be to view Messaging features like e-mail and Instant Messaging as one category to compare against other categories like Financial, which would includes bank sites, stock quotes, and financial news. Once you know which categories are working better than others, you can drill down into the category to see which features within that category are more important to your market.

Let's look at the usage of our mobile Internet portal from the last chapter using these new metrics. For this example, we will look at only the usage of heavy users to see what sites they are actually using within the portal.

In the table on the next page, we look at "categories" of sites to see whether there are any hidden successes in the features (sorted by attraction):

Category	Attraction (number of heavy users)	Stickiness (average visits per heavy user)	Usage (average time per heavy user)
Games	8,992	12.9	7m 00s
Downloads	5,103	14.0	20m 25s
Messaging	3,893	14.5	21m 09s
Sports	2,563	15.4	7m 30s
Adult	2,447	19.8	11m 56s
Entertainment	2,242	12.5	21m 56s
Chat	2,177	28.8	1h 17m 52s
Portals	1,948	11.3	13m 32s
Search	1,587	6.1	25m 31s
News	749	11.8	7m 57s
Weather	505	9.6	3m 55s
Horoscopes	311	13.8	5m 07s
Gambling	278	6.5	4m 18s
Commerce	235	8.7	10m 57s
Traffic	61	8.5	2m 56s
Travel	0	0.0	0s
Finance	0	0.0	0s
Banking	0	0.0	0s

Do you see the hidden key feature? It isn't Games, which has the highest number of users, as Games has fairly low usage and mediocre stickiness. It is Chat, which has the most stickiness (average visits per user) and the most usage (average time per user). The only problem with Chat is that it has a very low attraction, so it gets buried in the table.

The *Consumer Behavior Bubble Chart*

Studying tables of data to find anomalies is tedious and error prone. Instead, we use the *Consumer Behavior Bubble Chart*:

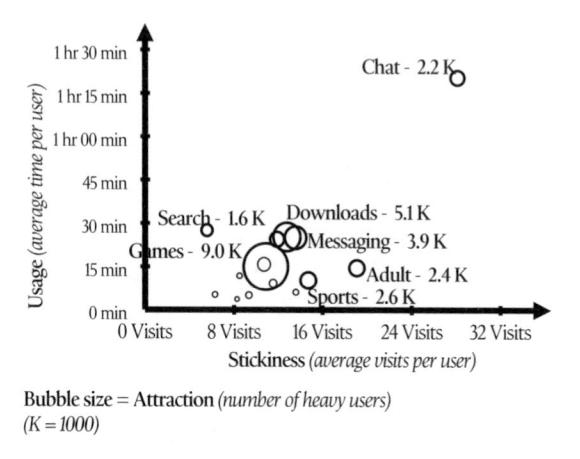

Bubble size = **Attraction** *(number of heavy users)*
(K = 1000)

The *Consumer Behavior Bubble Chart* above is a direct graphical representation of the table just shown.

The size of each bubble illustrates the attraction, or number of users that use each feature. The bigger the bubble, the more users are attracted to it. The x-axis shows the stickiness in terms of average visits per user. The farther right, the better the stickiness. The y-axis is the usage. The higher the bubble, the more minutes users use that feature has on average.

In the *Consumer Behavior Bubble Chart* above, you see the big bubble in the middle is Games—there are a lot of users attracted to it. However, for this operator, Games users are not returning often, and users don't spend a lot of time playing. This isn't to say that games are bad, it simply means that for this operator games are not working well to retain long-term users, either because the games they offer are not sticky, or because they are selling to a market segment who is not interested in games, like business people.

What really jumps out in this view of the data is Chat (in the upper right-hand corner). Notice that Chat has the highest usage and stickiness. It is a small bubble because it is hard to find in the operator's service offering, so most users never even know this service exists.

Other reasons for small bubbles are poorly named features, which users skip because they are unaware of what the features do.

If you are trying to see which features the users want, you need to normalize the attraction to account for features that are harder to get. This makes relative size of attraction more meaningful. We can do this for features in web sites or mobile Internet sites because we know what percentage of users are expected to click on every item and every sublevel. When you do this you will see what the users really want (because they are attracted to it) and can then compare that to the usage and stickiness of the feature to see whether the feature is delivering to that expectation.

How do we get more users to find your key feature? In the Internet and software world, it is actually quite easy. Instead of listing all the features as equal weight on the web page and leaving the navigation to the user, put your key features in key positions and bury the rest of the features.

For the mobile Internet example we are following, this means that the key services should be located in the key portal positions. Since we know the average first-time user will only try one or two features, and since we also know the user will tend to click only on the first items of the menu, we might make Chat our key feature and put it on the first slot of the first menu. Now more users will find this highly addictive and sticky feature.

This is exactly what our customers in Europe did, and it sparked Phase II adoption for mobile Internet in Europe, leaving the years of stalled adoption behind these operators.

View your product as a grocery store

To better illustrate these concepts, consider the non-technical analogy of a grocery store and the products they have to sell. Here you have the following activities for different types of products:

> **Advertise key attraction items in the window:** In a store, you would put your sale items on a sales banner in your store window. In a technology product, you will want to do the same, by marketing the features that you know will attract the most users to your product.

> Note: The features that attract users may not be the same ones that users buy. This is okay, because our goal is to attract users with our marketing. The product itself (like the store) may be organized differently to feature the high-value features up front (as required by earlier myths) so that we retain more users.

> **High-attraction items go in the back of the store:** Have you ever noticed that the key items you go to the store for (like milk, meat, and dairy products) are often located in the back of the store? They are not hidden, but they require you to walk past other products to get to them.

>> In our earlier mobile Internet example, Games and Downloads are key attraction features, but Chat is what keeps the users (it is stickier). We may decide to put Chat as the 1st item on the menu (because new us-

ers may not be sure what it is and you want them to try it), while we put Downloads and Games as the 2nd and 3rd item, knowing users are attracted because of these less sticky services.

Our goal is not to hide Downloads and Games (it is still prominent in the product), but to use their high attraction as a means to get the user to try our stickier features, which happen to be on the way to Downloads and Games.

Impulse items by the cash register: In a store, the candy and magazines are often by the cash register, which is the one place the store knows every user will go (and is thus the easiest place to put something the store wants you to find). The store hopes that while you are waiting you will find these other items and buy them.

In a technology product, you should also have your high-value features in the easiest place to find (as mentioned in the last chapter). Usually this means the high value must be in the first screen, the one place you know every user has to pass.

Focused product offerings: Stores tend to focus on specific products. Grocery stores focus on food products (like dairy, produce, and meat). Clothing stores focus on brands or types of clothing (like maternity, teenagers, or big and tall people).

Having everything in one store usually lowers the store's perceived value—and lowers its success as well. When you need a hammer, do you go to a hardware store or a grocery store? Most of us go to a hardware store, where we know we will *find* the hammer, find a better selection, and get better support.

In a technology product, you have to make similar sacrifices. Focus on your key features and don't try to be everything for everybody. Make sure the message to your target audience is clear and uncluttered, and win them over with a focused solution. This may mean removing features that are useless.

Now consider what the value of the low-performing services and features are to your product. The data we found for heavy users for our mobile Internet portal is telling:

At the bottom of the list of services in our mobile Internet portal are a few categories that have no usage and no stickiness for heavy users (Travel, Banking, Finance, and Traffic). These items also appeared in the bottom left of the bubble chart and had very small attraction.

Consider what happens when a first-time user stumbles into these features. We have already proven that no heavy users use these features, which means that in general you can expect that over time other users who go to these features will not likely return. Couple this with the knowledge that a first-time user will only try one or two features and you should realize that these features are actually putting your first-time users at risk.

The bad experience of poor services almost guarantees that these users won't return. If you can remove the features that are not used, there will be fewer bad first-time user experiences and your good features will ensure that they return. Deleting poorly performing features increases the odds of adoption occurring.

Deleting features has additional benefits. The product designer may insist that a feature has value, but if the data don't bear this out, the engineers and designers are wasting valuable development cycles on the wrong features. New products and startup companies don't have a lot of resources, so deleting or removing these features enables your company to focus better on what really works.

Let me give you a case from my early career of how I used this methodology to overtake a leading product with a poor product I inherited when I took my job:

> I was hired to run the Macintosh division of Central Point Software in 1990, which made consumer utility software like antivirus and disk repair. Our biggest competitor was Norton Utilities for the Macintosh from Symantec. Their product had been in the market longer and was generally better at most tasks. They had an 80% market share in our product category when I took the job.
>
> Central Point had MacTools, which had been in the market for several years and was in its second version. MacTools was failing against Norton. Our management at Central Point had the "more features" mentality, and by version 2 MacTools had collected over 10 utilities, including backup, antivirus, disk repair, disk optimization, floppy copying, fast file finder, file undelete, and others.
>
> We had more features than Norton, but we had fewer customers, a declining market share, and a lot less revenue.
>
> During the 5 years I worked at Central Point I reshaped the product to focus only on the key features consumers wanted and used (using registration cards, analysts visits, press reviews, customer surveys, and usability tests to determine which features mattered most). It turns out that only 4 products were used by most users: Antivirus, disk repair, backup, and disk optimization. I removed all other features and put all our resources into making these 4 key features the best possible.
>
> Disk repair was our "milk"—to use the grocery store analogy—as it attracted most of our users. But we prominently displayed disk optimization, backup, and antivirus on our main window as we knew it was our "candy," as they were

not why the product was purchased, but they were impulse items that kept users coming back (i.e., the stickiest, most visited features after purchase). So we engineered the disk repair to be the best in the business and focused solely on disk repair in our attraction campaigns (meetings with the press, advertisement, box design, etc.). This intense focus allowed us to build the best repair product, attract the most attention, and eventually to grow from 20% market share to over 60% market share for Macintosh utilities.

Looking at more current products, consider a similar story that I wasn't involved with but could have predicted easily:

> Yahoo! used to be the market leader for search engines, with over 90% of the market for this feature. As of the writing of this book they had a 23% market share, and they were not beaten by Microsoft, with the strongest name brand with MSN (11%)—they were beaten by a new company that offers their customers just the search feature: Google (46% market share).[*]

> How did Yahoo! lose their market share? Most people will tell you it is because Google is technically a better search engine. I'd argue that Google has a better search engine because of their single-focused approach.

> Google focused better than Yahoo! on their market in every way, from the customer experience to the marketing and engineering. It was destined to win in the consumer market.

> The average user has no idea why or how Google is a better search engine technically. It certainly is not the technical excellence of the product that is winning—it is the single-minded focus on search. Google creates both a feeling of simplicity, completeness, and speed, all critical features in the minds of consumers.

---

[*] Market share data from SearchEngineWatch, January 24, 2006.

When you go to Yahoo!, how many features do you see? Fortunately, they still keep search focused in the center, but the feature creep of Yahoo! is staggering (I counted over 30 features just on their home page). How many features do you think the average first-time user uses on Yahoo!?

When you go to Google, how many features do you see? I found just one: Search. There is a button called "More tools..." that leads to additional search-related added-value features. With Google, users have no bad experiences and no distractions. Google owns their users and are stealing users from other companies due to its ability to sacrifice features.

Yahoo!'s attempt at additional ARPU has caused it to be the "Jack of all trades" and to lose users easily. Yahoo! could delete all features but the 3 or 4 that really matter (offloading these features to submenus), reduce clutter in the user's experience, and probably regain leadership and significantly increase revenue potential. If the other features have true value, they could use smart detection and make the features they know an individual uses available on the home page without having the full menu.

The trend today is for Google to capitalize on its market share (we already see sponsored links and advertising on the results page). The challenge for Google will be to ensure that their revenue activities and new features don't impair the user and that the search results are still relevant.

Conclusion: Users want a few good features

I have two last thoughts in closing this chapter. First, I hope you have learned here that the basic role of features in new products is to capture users through value. I hope I showed you here why too many features can devalue your product, affect the focus at your company, and lead to poor experiences for your users.

The second thought is a different way to view the features in your product. Consider the following maxim that comes from a consumer's viewpoint of your product:

> Your product or service is only as good as its worst features or service.

This is usually the exact opposite of the viewpoint of the person designing the product, who would like to judge the product based on its best features.

But if users have poor experiences with your product (because they stumble into the poor features), then they will have a poor impression of your entire product. Consumers are not forgiving. Take away those poor experiences (i.e., the features that either don't add value or impede usage) and users will focus on the good experiences (i.e., the features that *do* add value). This leads to success for your users and for you as your consumers adopt your product quicker.

Why we fail

When *Five Myths of Consumer Behavior* was originally written, this chapter was called "Introduction" and it came before the actual myths. At the time, we felt we needed to help the reader understand why product designers failed before introducing the myths. We wanted to "set the stage" for the best possible success in your reading experience.

What we really did was to break several of the very myths we were writing about in this book. When this book was evaluated as we would evaluate a product for "first-time user experience," "stickiness," and navigational flow, it failed its user. Once we recognized that this chapter, "Why we fail," is a "feature" of our product (the book), then we also recognized that the 5 chapters describing myths were the true "value" of the book. We can't hope you find our value, so we moved the myths up front—not because this chapter isn't important (it is), but because the true value had to be shared first. Now this chapter is even better because we have the context of the myths behind us.

So, why do we fail?

We fail because the consumer's mindset is in contrast to our own mindset as we design products. We fail because we can't predict what consumers will think while they use our products. We fail because we get too close to our products, which is too far from our consumers. We design products by our principles and fight to find ways to resist our instincts and come back to the reality our consumers' experience.

Study your consumers' behaviors

To get to the root of why consumers try, buy, use, and become addicted to technology products and services, you must first be skilled in studying people and their behavior. Watch your consumers and learn about the triggers that cause them to make up or change their minds. Study their "frame of mind" or "mental state" at each trigger point in the product's life cycle.

For a traditional retail product, this means watching users as they consider your product:

> If you are selling aspirin, it is valuable to know why a person stopped in front of the aspirin display (he had a headache, or a sign offering 50% off caught his eye)—what *triggered* him to stop in the first place. After stopping, you see him reach for a package—what triggered that? He selects gel tabs—why not capsules? Why do some people put the product back, while others put it in their basket?

In the technology and Internet world, this same analysis can be done by examining the transactions as users browse or use your product:

> Look at the electronic transactions recorded by your users to tell you which users are finding each feature, which users are deciding to use a particular feature (and what features they use the most), and which users don't follow through with a feature (and, more importantly, at which step they stopped

using it). If you study many individuals, you will soon find predictable patterns driving their behavior and their successes or failures with your product.

These data analyses are the cornerstone of the services we perform for our clients who are trying to achieve consumer success. We have analyzed millions of users to build statistical models of their interactions with technology products. The results have repeatedly proved why the five myths described in this book are the root cause of bad product implementation.

With the data available, you can deconstruct the user's path to see where the barriers are that trigger success or failure. It's all about the consumer's state of mind, which changes as users flow from their first visit to becoming addicted users of your product.

For example, consider your state of mind while reading this book:

Originally, upon purchasing and first reading this book, you were likely to be in a particular state of mind depending on the reason you bought this book:

You want or need to better understand consumers to help improve your own product

You find books on consumer behavior entertaining

A class or employer required that you read this book

If you bought the book because you have a product you are trying to develop, then you most likely began reading this book in a learning mode: Either Defensive-Learning mode (if you have already designed your product) or Buying-Learning mode (if you are still researching how to design the product). The difference is due to how much work you have already invested or how much information you have already collected. The more effort you have already invested in a product, the more likely you will challenge the ideas in this book (your state of mind is to defend your past efforts); the less effort, the more open-minded you will be.

If you bought this book to be entertained, you began in Entertained mode (and we hope that we managed to move you into Buying-Learning mode as you read it, to help your long-term recollection of the key principles).

Finally, if you are forced to read the book for a class or job, you probably started out in Working mode, approaching the book as an assignment or job (with no real commitment or opinion for or against its content). In this case, we hope that we switched you into Entertained mode, because the only thing that is worse than being forced to read a book is being forced to read a boring book.

All of these modes are critical to helping you understand your consumer's state of mind. They help you to remove your own influences from the experience and objectively find and solve product problems.

Example: Becoming addicted to the Internet

Try to think of how a new customer approaches your product. What interactions do you witness? Is the customer in the right state of mind at the right time to progress from a prospective user to an addicted user? Why is he looking at your product? Are there defenses in place? Is he easily distracted or discouraged?

As an example, consider the average person's consumer adoption path to the Internet. I use this example since most of us are now addicted to the Internet, but as a product it is young enough that some of us can still remember how it was introduced into our lives and how we made the decision to use it (unlike the telephone or TV, which we were raised with and accept without question):

We first heard about the Internet, probably on the news or in a magazine, in the mid to late 90s. Most people started in Curiosity-Learning mode ("What is this? Is this some type of research tool?") or Defensive-Learning mode ("I don't need it," "I already get my stock quotes from the paper," "I buy my books at a store.")

At some point later, a friend showed you how he was using the Internet and what you saw were things like e-mail, Yahoo!, or Amazon.com. Before watching your friend use it, you may have had a debate about why you didn't care to use it (Defensive-Learning mode) or you confessed your curiosity by asking questions (Curiosity-Learning mode). But once he started showing you, you jumped to Buying-Learning mode, trying to learn and understand what you were seeing and trying to determine whether it was right for you.

Most of us saw enough value in that first demo to try the Internet again later on our own. After discovering a real service, like e-mail, we became everyday users, using the Internet in Working mode or Entertained mode, thinking only about the result, not the mechanics.

Understanding these modes helps you to empathize with consumers when you don't have the opportunity for one-on-one interactions.

The key to failure: "First-principle" design

If you are an executive, marketer, or engineer, you need to know your users' states of mind as they interact with your products or services. As soon as you lose touch with your consumers' state of mind, you lose touch with good decision-making.

Most of the key myths reported in this book stem from the designer assuming that users will be willing to perform something that is unnatural for their state of mind (i.e., it goes against fundamental consumer behavior principals). Designers fall into this trap because they are too close to their product, while their consumers know nothing, entering with a blank slate. This, in turn, causes the designer to make first-principle decisions, which are decisions that are assumed without proper consumer visualization, consumer testing, and research.

First-principle design, for example, says that a web-hosted software service needs a registration process as a first step. However, most users stop here. Putting a barrier like this in front of your product's value will always limit your consumer base. Few users are in the proper state of mind to go through these types of steps before trying your product.

It is better to give limited access to the product without registration and ask for information only as needed as the user accesses more advanced services (or ask only for information that is truly needed to try the product). It is also better to require only what is really needed to advance to the next step, rather than a 5-page registration that provides dozens of potential opportunities for the user to either quit or become frustrated with your company's poor design and decision process.

The same theory—using the consumer's state of mind to ease him into the purchase—and poor first-principle thinking can affect consumer products as well as services. My coauthor Ali provides an example:

> Ali's little son, Christopher, had some pocket money and dragged his dad to the local toy store (okay—Ali didn't take too much dragging). There are many different toys in the store and all look attractive on the shelf. Almost every toy needs batteries nowadays and, of course, the toys are wrapped up in their boxes waiting for some lucky kid to open them and pester his parents to put the batteries in.

On this day, however, we learned how batteries can add revenue instead of costs. Christopher spotted a cuddly talking gorilla, which is interesting—but no more interesting than anything else. But the gorilla he's looking at has a big button on the front that makes the gorilla talk! (and what kid can resist pressing any button, as we all know when there is a 3-year-old on the elevator). Christopher tries that, while it's still on the shelf in the box, and it makes him laugh—he thinks it's great!

Which toy do you think Christopher walked out of the store with? What's more, his dad purchased more batteries because the helpful sales associate convinced him that the batteries installed were only for demonstration and that they might not last long—and wouldn't Christopher be upset if they ran out. Do you think Christopher's "spare change" covered the cost of the toy and the batteries? Of course, as any dad knows, the spare change is always "exactly what it costs" to the child.

Funny thing is, the batteries still haven't run out, and Christopher is still playing with that gorilla. Sure, it cost the manufacturer to provide batteries and design the packaging so the product can be tried. However, the value (in this case revenue) to the manufacturer is that Christopher walked out of the store with the gorilla and not another toy.

First-principle design tells the toy manufacturer not to include batteries because they add costs. First-principle design tells the toy resellers to resist stocking toys with batteries because they decrease battery sales at the counter, causing loss of revenue and margins. However, state of mind research shows that children will buy what they can touch and hear firsthand, which leads to the sale of a higher-priced toy (this makes the manufacturer happy), and the retailer is still selling more batteries.

Conclusion: We fail because we don't empathize

Don't lose sight of your product's true consumer. Learn what their state of mind is and how you can logically analyze and avoid costly barriers to success. Don't make assumptions and act on them without first thinking through the implications empathically with the user.

How we can succeed

This chapter presents a process for designing new products that will enable rapid consumer adoption. You can use this process whether you are already well into your product's life cycle or you are just beginning to develop a new consumer product.

First, let me share my own secret to success as a consumer behavior expert:

> I question absolutely everything, assume nothing, and measure everything. I don't now, nor have I ever, looked at the world and accepted it for what others told me it is. I approach the world as the constant observer, creating and testing every hypothesis and reducing observations down to new logic that can sometimes fly in the face of common knowledge or passed-down wisdom.

> When applying these philosophies to help a company sell a consumer product, I deconstruct the consumer's mindset

from past behavior and question every interaction, every
passed-down bit of corporate wisdom, and rehash every
product design decision that assumes a user's behavior. I
measure users' behaviors with whatever tools are available
and then rebuild a new model that ensures users will pass
through every gate needed to become loyal followers. I never
stop observing, questioning, testing, and inventing.

To be successful with consumer products, you will need to start
questioning your own product and marketing decisions. You
will also need to remove yourself as a potential user (you know
too much) and find other ways to analyze your consumers to
find the truth. Don't rely on passed-down wisdom or practices
that "worked in the past." The most common myths are described in this book, but every product is different and you will
need to stay alert to discovering new assumptions that are relevant to your company and your products. You will also need to
find ways to test those assumptions.

Let me give you an example of an everyday situation that is
riddled with past influences and assumptions that can lead to
an improper outcome.

I'd like a noisy hotel room, please

I'm talking about hotel rooms, and why many consumers ask
for a "quiet" room on check-in. Here is my practice:

> In my job, I travel a lot (a whole lot). When I check into a ho-
> tel, I always request the "noisiest room on the road."

> I used to ask for a "quiet" room, just like almost every other
> hotel guest in the world. However, I rarely got a good night's
> sleep. As I began to travel more, I decided to test my prior as-
> sumption that asking for a quiet room will ensure a good
> night's sleep. I tried many types of rooms and started evaluat-

ing my experiences and sleep patterns. I soon found I liked "noisy" rooms better.

Soon thereafter, I started requesting a noisy room intentionally. I found that this removed me from the consumer pool (my practice is the opposite of others), which allowed me to better analyze consumer behavior in hotels.

Now I interact with the staff and other hotel guests on different terms. Sometimes I get giggles in response to my request (the person assumes I'm joking); sometimes I get the wrong room (the person doesn't believe me and thinks I'm being sarcastic); but most often, I'm asked to explain my logic (they have to know why I made the request). However, almost every time, I get two things everyone really wants in a hotel room stay: The best service the hotel can give, and a great night's sleep.

Before reading on, re-read the story above and stop to think for a moment about my practice of asking for a noisy room. Can you find the answer as to why my asking for a noisy room gives me both great service and a great night's sleep?

See if you can remove or resist your own brain's insistence that my statement above is a riddle, a joke, a trick, or a lie.

Finding a process for success

Before I tell you the secret of the noisy hotel room, I want to share the process I use to find success with consumers when they use technology products. We will get back to the hotel room riddle at the end of this chapter.

The diagram that follows shows the *Rapid Consumer Adoption Process*. It is used for creating and improving technology products or services that are consumer successes:

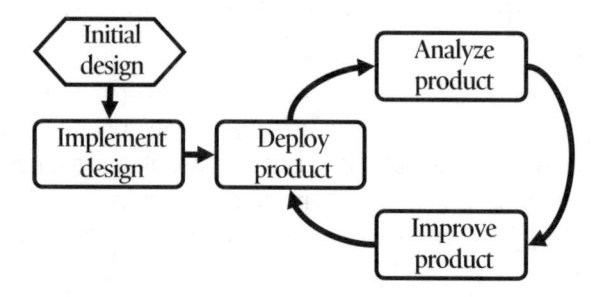

The *Rapid Consumer Adoption Process* is as simple as it looks, but it is amazing how many companies skip or short-circuit the various phases and fall back on first-principle design. For these companies, building and evolving a product become an exercise in guesswork instead of a planned process for success.

Initial design phase

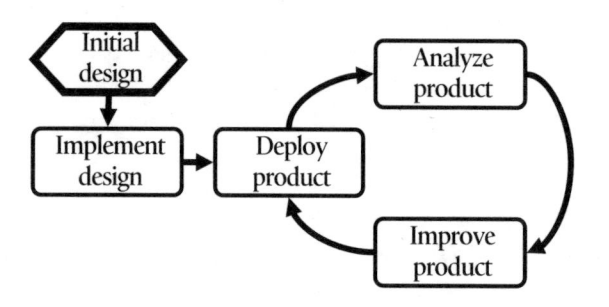

Okay, so you are obviously in entrepreneurial mode—after all, you are about to design and build a product that you hope will become a runaway consumer success. A common attribute of entrepreneurs is that they are risk-takers (why else would they risk their careers trying to invent a new consumer product?).

I've seen this risk-taking attitude run out of control with many entrepreneurs. Every decision they have to make to build a new product is a guess, and they become very comfortable designing the entire product based on first principles. I admit that many decisions will require best guesses, but does that mean all caution should be thrown out? Some first-principle decisions and guesswork will bear fruit, but if you look at inventors who have eventually achieved commercial success, you'll usually find some significant work on analysis as well. It was Thomas Edison who said "Genius is one percent inspiration and ninety-nine percent perspiration"—and he was certainly qualified to make that comment.

In fact, if you really want a success, you will focus on trying to reduce risks. The best way to reduce risk is to make honest comparisons about your market with other similar markets. However, as we mentioned in the first myth, you will need to research the key success factors of that market in Phase I adoption.

This extra information, coupled with good research into your own market, will help you to at least look at the new product with open eyes. All of the external research, however, is only a part of reducing risks, because you will still have to make many guesses.

The next most important thing is to focus on a small set of key features that solve real problems. Similar markets will have very mature and rich feature sets, which is appropriate for a Phase III product. But, Myth 5 showed that when you are in Phase I, too many features can potentially stall adoption. You will have plenty of time while your product is growing in the market to fill out the feature set and, in most cases, the features you think are important now probably are not.

To get your features right, then, you need a way to focus your efforts. The best way I've found to do this is to take an extremely hard look at the problem your product intends to solve and document it carefully to truly describe what you are trying to do. Then test that problem statement with real users who appear to meet your initial customer segment definition to see if they, too, see that as a real problem, and whether your solution fits.

Think of the big consumer successes and try formulating an initial problem statement. What was the real problem, for example, that the original concept of the personal computer solved? What about the Internet, the VCR, the laptop computer, or the mobile phone? What fundamental problems were these systems trying to solve?

It is often hard to determine the original problem statement for successful products because we only know of them as successes. But all of these products began their adoption successes with a narrowly defined market segment of users and a focused set of features that solved the original user problem very well.

Let's look at the case of the original personal computers:

> The original problem being solved wasn't "Recipes for Mom." "Mom" is not an early adopter of technology products (well, at least my mom isn't). The original problem was smarter business computers for desktops at corporations. "Personal" didn't originally mean "consumer," it meant "not mainframe" or shared computer access.

> Putting a computer on the desktop distributed computing capacity, allowed offline (off the mainframe) computations, and enabled businesses who were early adopters of computer capacity to more efficiently run their businesses.

> With the advent of the word processor and spreadsheet programs, the PC spread to all businesses, even small ones. The original problem could have been stated as "Give business dependable computer access for offline work," as sharing mainframe time wasn't dependable for businesses.

The original PC vendors noticed quickly that the faster they made these desktop machines, the more they sold. In fact, they found several key success factors to driving their marketplace: Speed, more memory, and more disk space. For years these were the only features that influenced a purchasing decision.

Eventually, the speed, memory, and software matured to the point that the consumer population began adopting, rushing it through Phase II adoption in a few years. Now that this market is in Phase III, there are many other detailed features that buyers consider, like built-in DVD players, CD burners, Ethernet access, etc. This richness today is a sign of how well this market has matured and has created the ARPU opportunities that often exist in Phase III of the adoption cycle.

Now look at how this differs from laptop computers, which may have looked like the same market as the PC, but in reality solved a different problem and had a different set of key success factors:

Soon after the PC was introduced, designers discovered another important market problem: People need computers while they are traveling. This sparked early successes like Compaq's original "portable computer" (it was about as big as my desktop computer at work, but it had a handle on it).

Soon companies realized that the smaller the portable and the better the battery life, the more they sold (and these became the key success factors for this new market). Eventually, consumer-grade models were developed, and now "laptop" is a consumer product that is in its early Phase III growth cycle, with many critical features for success, including wireless access, USB ports, good audio, great battery life, DVD players, etc.

Now that laptops are in Phase III adoption, users are addicted, so they put up with inconveniences for more power. If you have watched portable computers over time, you may have noticed that "small" has saturated, and most standard laptops are now a bit bigger than they used to be and have more features that these addicted users find as critical and worthy of the extra size and weight.

Now let's look at a market where the key success factors weren't uncovered: The personal digital assistant (PDA).

The PDA continues to lag in Phase I adoption because the key success factors are not well understood. The original Apple Newton was a glorious product if you could stomach the size and weight. It is a dead product now, killed by the engineers who added too many features too early in the adoption life cycle.

The second major release of the Apple Newton shipped in a bigger and heavier form, which showed a complete lack of understanding of what key success factors to optimize. The engineers focused on new features, which required the extra memory, extra battery life, and weight.

So what happened? A competitor saw Apple's lack of understanding of their market and came out with a smaller PDA with fewer features, the Palm Pilot (now called simply the Palm). The Palm stole the market in no time flat, putting the Apple Newton out of business, even though the Palm had significantly fewer features, and even had an unnatural handwriting recognition system.

What did Palm's engineers do with their success? They forged ahead on the feature mania trail as well, with their next upgrade being no smaller than the first. But, in this case someone discovered the mistake and came out with a line of smaller units with fewer features, allowing adoption to begin to take hold.

Then why doesn't everyone own a PDA?

> The PDA market still isn't a wide consumer success. Yes, many people have bought and used PDAs, but almost everyone eventually quits using them. This market still hasn't discovered the true key to longevity (stickiness) with their users.
>
> If I had to guess, I'd say the failure of PDAs is due to disrespect for user data. These devices still expect users to back up their PDAs to their PCs (who backs up anything anymore?). Backing up is a power user solution (I'll bet that 90% of PDA users either don't back up or rarely back up). Having the back up feature in place, PDA manufacturers justify purchasing memory that isn't safe when the battery dies or the unit is otherwise disrupted.
>
> So PDA manufacturers save their money by buying cheaper memory and continue to ignore their key barrier to long-term adoption. Ask anyone who has ever used a PDA for a while and then quit, and they will tell you that the day they quit was the day they lost all of their data and didn't have a backup.

We can walk through every consumer success and see the same *Consumer Adoption S-Curve* growth take place, where in Phase I the focus is on a narrow market segment that is likely to adopt, key success factors are identified, and those factors are optimized until the product becomes consumer grade, sparking Phase II adoption.

To find your product's key success factors:

Narrowly define a single market segment that is likely to have early adopters for your product.

Define a true problem that a market segment perceives as needing to be solved.

Use these definitions to theorize key success factors (e.g., size, speed, or memory capacity).

In summary, below are the steps to designing a successful new product for consumer markets:

Define a clear problem statement: Your problem statement is your key to delivering the right value to your consumers by solving a compelling problem for a real need in a real market segment.

Define a targeted market segment: Although you see your product as a Phase III success, new consumers will take much longer to find that same value. Select an initial market segment that is narrow enough that (1) you can focus on it and (2) will exhibit tendencies to drive early adoption (i.e., stickiness). If your initial market segment is "everybody," you are trying to jump directly to Phase III and your product will languish.

Research the market: Try to find out what other products this market is supporting and why. What made these products successful? Is this market likely to drive early adoption (young people and business users typically have a tendency to buy new technology for entertainment or to solve real problems).

Postulate your key success factors: Try to think through your future success factors that will result in a consumer-grade product. The better you are at postulating this, the better you will be at confirming these factors later once your product ships.

Derive your features from your key success factors: The key success factors, the problem statement, and the initial market segment will drive your feature definitions. This may mean a stronger focus on convenience and ease of use and less focus on new extensions and new features.

Write your initial product specification: Now you can specify your product. You have the features, market segment, key success factors, and the core problem you are solving.

Implementing the initial design

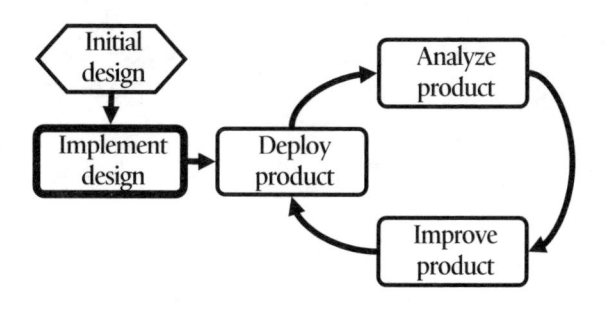

Now comes the hard part. The designers have studied their own market and similar markets; they have defined a good problem statement; they have identified their initial market segment and tested it, even informally, to ensure the problem is real; and they have identified initial key success factors. Finally, they reduced all of this work down into a single specification document.

This initial design specification is handed to the engineers for implementation. The engineers turn the specification into a work list of features.

What is wrong with this process? The problem lies in the last step, where the specification is handed to engineers. The product has been reduced to a list of features, and the real core value of the problem being solved, the market definition, and the key success factors are not properly prioritized and communicated.

Engineers tend to solve the minor feature tweaks using themselves as the audience. As we showed in Myth 3, engineers are exactly the wrong people to make these decisions (they are power users).

The key to success in the implementation phase is not only to share with engineering the market problem, segmentation information, and key success factors, but to show how features are prioritized and the factors that surround those definitions. Engineers are smart people, but you need to give them a basis for making good decisions. Keep the spirit of the original problem being solved alive and eliminate risks during this phase. Give your engineers a copy of this book as well, to help them understand how to remain in context.

Although I don't personally work with Google, it appears that they have a good process for keeping their vision alive:

> Simply by using Google it is clear that there are some very strong core values at work behind the scene. I'd bet my bottom dollar that there is a passionate visionary and consumer advocate who insists every day that the product stay simple.

> How many times do you think a newly hired Google engineer or marketing person suggested putting more features on the Google home page? I can only imagine the cultural lectures and indoctrination these newcomers get in their first few weeks.

> We, the consumers, thank that person, and remain loyal to Google.

I want to emphasize prioritization one more time. Avoid having too many useless features (Myth 5). Avoid implementing or optimizing the wrong features. Identify the product's key features and always schedule these for first implementation. Trying to build all features with the same weight will cause problems when it is time to ship the product if the key features are incomplete and the wrong features are overengineered. With no time left, last-minute decisions to drop features should never affect the core value of your product or its key features.

To review, the following steps have to be completed successfully in the implementation phase of your product's life cycle:

Share your fundamentals with engineering: Don't just give a feature specification to engineering, give them all of the knowledge about the targeted market segment, the problem being solved, and the key success factors that drove the design of those features. Don't risk your product's success by hoping engineers have your knowledge about your market. Make sure everyone can make good decisions during the product implementation phase. Make it so easy that even Homer Simpson can use it.

Prioritize your features: Make sure you prioritize the features before giving them to engineering. Assume that schedules will be tight at the end, and ensure that key features are done first before this time comes.

Train your engineers in the *Rapid Consumer Adoption Process:* I highly recommend that you train your engineering team in the concepts from this chapter (and indeed, this entire book). You want them to understand the process you are using to obtain quick success, and you want them to avoid the myths mentioned in this book. Most engineers will be glad to understand where you are coming from so that their day-to-day decisions can be made in the same spirit as that which drove your original design.

Deploy the product

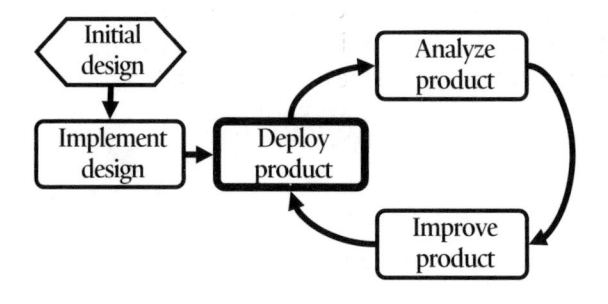

To deploy a newly implemented product, or to deploy a newly improved product (following the improvement cycle on the right of the diagram), requires that the product be properly tested to ensure that it has no bugs. Unfortunately, this deployment process often excludes one of the most important identifiers of bugs in a product: Usability flaws.

I've seen millions of dollars go into multiple versions of a product stuck in Phase I without ever going through a solid usability test. Usability has probably killed more products in the marketplace quicker than Priority 1 bugs have (known crashes in products). Don't let your engineers consider a feature complete just because it doesn't crash. If 99% of users don't use it, who cares if it crashes 6 levels down? The crashes all eventually get fixed, but by putting usability as Priority 2 or Priority 3, you guarantee your product will still fail.

Usability testing is to a marketer as bug fixing is to an engineer. You designed the product on first principles—now you need to test those principles. Just as engineers test for flaws in their programming, you must test for flaws in your consumer design (or risk an equivalent failure). A professional engineer won't ship until the important bugs are fixed, and you shouldn't ship until the important usability flaws are resolved.

Consider one mobile Internet portal my wife used several years ago. In an improvement phase they took Yahoo! off of their home page and put it in a folder called Portals, along with the mobile Internet sites from AOL and MSN.

This made sense to the marketing people in a first-principle design and with their deep knowledge of the industry.

Prior to this change, my wife was a regular user of the service, primarily because of Yahoo! e-mail. A few months after the change, I noticed that my wife wasn't using the service anymore.

I asked her why, and she said, "They deleted Yahoo! from the phone."

So I looked at the phone with her and, being a power user myself, I naturally went into Portals and found Yahoo! She said, "Oh, I didn't know what 'Portals' meant."

The word "Portal" is not a consumer term, and it made me wonder how many other users this operator lost by not usability testing this design. Another solution would have been to perform a business intelligence analysis before and after the new portal design, which would have shown a significant drop-off of regular users.

If you consider the loss of a user as a Priority 1 bug, then both crashes and usability problems will become Priority 1. If you don't do this, consumers will decide for you with their unforgiving "No" vote.

Usability testing

One last point is important about usability testing, which is often misunderstood. You need to do this with an eye toward finding the problems, not proving the design is correct.

One common mistake is to perform focus group tests as a substitute for usability testing. In focus groups, users are walked through a product demonstration and then asked what they think. There is so much educating and steering by the facilitator that very little is learned about what is wrong with the product. Focus group users are in the wrong state of mind (Defensive-Learning mode instead of Buying-Learning mode or Curiosity-Learning mode). You want to watch your users struggle now so you can improve, not prove your first-principle design is great.

Never demonstrate a product or even help users with the product during a usability test. A good facilitator will ask the user to solve some key problems that come directly from the problem statement that originally led to the design of the product. He will not help the user—he will watch the user and keep encouraging him to try to find the solution to the problem.

Don't use your own employees as test subjects (they know too much). Instead, select candidates from your defined market segmentation, as it is better to learn from real potential users (especially those who have never heard of or know your product) who will show what problems first-time users will experience. Test with users from your current install base only when you have a strong product and are simply making improvements to the product (such as when you are in Phase III adoption). Either way, you should never help these users solve the problems.

Watching users struggle with your product will be enlightening for your team. You need to see how little patience users have when solving problems with your product. It can be disheartening to watch a frustrated user unable to use your product, but the good news is you now know why the product isn't succeeding. Every usability test I've conducted has uncovered some shocking surprises and design flaws.

The best thing about usability testing is that it only takes about 5–10 users before you see clear patterns. The small sample of users may seem statistically insignificant to your staff, so get them to watch the tests with you. After they watch 9 out of 10 users fail to find Yahoo! e-mail because it is under the Portal menu, there will be no argument that the test was beneficial and the problems found must be fixed.

The good news is that most problems found in usability testing can be easily fixed without major design or architectural changes to the product. In fact, fixing most usability flaws is easier than fixing normal bugs.

Below is a list of the key steps to follow during the final deployment phases of a product:

Ensure key features were implemented correctly: Go back to your original key success factor decisions and key problem statement and review the product against these concepts. Make sure users can solve these problems easily.

Perform a usability test as soon as the product is stable: You can almost always do this in parallel to the engineering QA cycle because product bugs will have less effect on a usability test (users usually don't get that deep in a 1-hour usability test). It is good to invite engineers to watch usability tests so they can see the importance of fixing the new problems; it also helps them to visualize users for future decisions.

Analyze the product

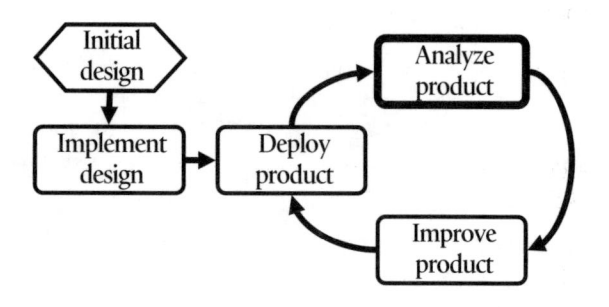

The Deployment phase contained a usability test. Most of the easy-to-fix issues were fixed before deployment, but some issues will likely require more effort than time permitted, so these issues go into the Analysis phase of the product's life cycle. There will be other leftover issues after shipping a product, including early feedback from your customer support, early feedback from the press and analysts, and engineering issues (such as poor architectures or missing features that couldn't be included in the last release).

All of these issues, as well as your original product vision, problem statement, and key success factors, should be collected and used as input into a proper business intelligence analysis. Now is the best time to determine how many of those first-principle decisions and guesses are playing out in the real market. Were the features you emphasized the real sticky features with real users? What features are your users being attracted to the most? Are these features delivering on the user's expectations?

Myth 4 and Myth 5 both show how to perform this business analysis correctly to find out where first-time users are going and where regular users and heavy users are staying.

If you are analyzing a product that has just been improved, make sure you have business intelligence data from before the deployment for comparison.

In summary, the Analysis phase should include the following steps:

Collect leftover engineering and usability issues: Catalog the issues that were not resolved in the deployment phase, including issues that couldn't be fixed or features that weren't deployed.

Collect external feedback: Catalog the issues from customer support, your retail channel, sales figures, and press and analysts' feedback on your product.

Review your original product goals: Catalog your original problem statement, key success factors, and market segmentation.

Perform a business intelligence analysis to test this data: Review all of the data collected above against real performance by real users. This business intelligence should be done to isolate first-time users from regular users and heavy users. Test every assumption and try to find new factors to include in the next round of improvements.

Improve the product

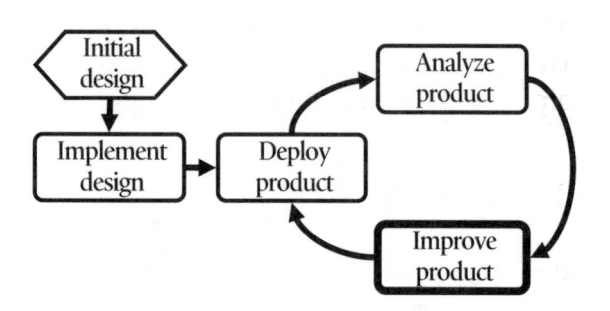

The Improvement phase of your product's life cycle should be approached in the same way as the Initial Design phase, but now you should have more data to help make better decisions. Your goal now is to continue to refine the core success factors while abandoning the failed features or ideas that were applied in the last cycle.

Use the feedback from the Analysis phase of the product's life cycle to drive a fresh new definition of the core problem statement for your product and a new set of key success factors.

Also, see if there is a more accelerated market segment than you originally defined. Maybe features you never thought were important are being used heavily by a market segment that is a better candidate for early adoption growth focus. If this is the case, don't be afraid to change your target segment.

After refining your fundamentals, you can now select the key features that require the most effort in this next round. Don't be afraid to delete features during this phase, because those poorly performing features are probably hurting your adoption instead of helping it.

You may find that some key features will require an expert re-design to make it more usable. Hire true consumer adoption experts and consultants to help provide these new designs. Watching experts improve one or two features will help your team learn better how to be consumer adoption experts themselves. The rapid adoption process can only work if you are always learning, and always refining your product.

The real hotel situation

Here is the conclusion to the noisy hotel room story:

> The real issue isn't that *I* believe you sleep better in a noisy room, but rather that *you* think hotels have quiet rooms. Once you accept that hotels don't have quiet rooms, you need to decide what type of noisy room you want.

> For example, if you ask for a "quiet" room at a hotel, you get a room facing a wall or atrium. This room is considered quiet because there is no street noise. But is it really quiet? What about the late-night traveler who comes in next door at 1 am and turns on his TV? Or the person next door who gets up at 5 am? Does housekeeping count as noise in the morning? Does your paper flopping down at 4:30 am by your front door wake you? Does any of this count as noise? You bet!

> But, you may argue, car noise just makes a moderately noisy room noisier. I agree. But what is important is how your brain processes total quiet (what you get at home in the countryside) with occasional interruptions (the supposedly quiet rooms at a hotel) versus how your brain deals with constant noise like traffic (white noise).

> The main reason I can't sleep in a hotel isn't that I have a problem falling asleep (especially if I'm jet-lagged), it's a problem of staying asleep with the odd hotel noises. The white noise of traffic doesn't bother me when falling asleep—I actually find it soothing.

After I fall asleep with the road noise, it becomes white noise, and, if it is noisy enough, the other hotel noises get washed out along with it. Just as you can dream you are running but your legs don't move, your brain can also turn off your hearing if that's what it takes to let you sleep (like sailors in a submarine who don't hear the engines anymore). It is the traffic noise that triggers turning off your hearing, allowing *uninterrupted* sleep, which is the real goal after all, isn't it?

It also helps if you can see the other advantages in having a room next to the road. If you ask for a quiet room and are given one near the road, you probably stew over the inconsiderate hotel staff—a negative state of mind that won't promote peaceful sleep.

However, if you asked for the room next to the road, you accepted that room as a good thing (your expectations are met, not underdelivered), which makes falling asleep with the noise even easier. I see other benefits as well, such as something to look at outside my window, connecting me with the local community. This makes my hotel stays less lonely and comforts me while I'm working in my room. This will only happen if I get a room on the street.

I like good service, and my habit of asking for a noisy room usually makes me very recognizable to the hotel staff by triggering a state of mind change for them. This mode switch causes them to look up and remember me, rather than check me in as an unknown face. I become a memorable "regular," even if I've only been to the hotel a few times, and as a regular guest I get their best service.

In conclusion, never assume anything, and keep your mind open to new situations or thinking. Usually the best solutions for making a product successful require finding odd or unusual patterns that initially don't coincide with the design goals or corporate philosophies. Consumer behavior is the result of user decisions, not your desires for the offering. Look closely at the results of that usability study or business intelligence analysis with a fresh and questioning mind.

Conclusion: We can succeed

True adoption can be obtained if your marketing and engineering teams can embrace the *Rapid Consumer Adoption Process* as well as embrace the knowledge that consumers do not follow intuitive behavior patterns. They need to understand the myths of consumer behavior presented in this text, and they need to stop first-principle design. Stop revolutionizing the product and start evolving it.

Once deployed, the first version of your product will need to be tested and retested objectively. Ensure that your staff is committed to a continuous cycle of improvement based on factual knowledge (real business intelligence) and complete data testing, not guesswork. The guessing stops as soon as the first version of the product ships. Don't let your consumer adoption stagnate in Phase I. Perform an initial usability test and business intelligence analysis and avoid poor decisions that will delay adoption—a risk your company cannot afford.

If you deploy the *Rapid Consumer Adoption Process* correctly and objectively, you should quickly find ways to double and triple your marketplace.

Acknowledgements

I'd like to acknowledge the people who have supported my consumer research over the years. First, let me thank Alastair France, Mark Knisely, and Jeremy Weinstein, who have all helped in immeasurable ways to implement sophisticated business intelligence technologies used to track consumer usage.

I'd like to thank all of the customers I've worked with throughout the years for their support and willingness to allow us to work directly with them to solve their consumer adoption problems, particularly those individuals who spearheaded changes needed within their companies.

Thank you Jennifer Gardner for your help on the many edits to get this work published.

Finally, I'd like to thank my wife, Diane Smethers, for her help in writing this book. I'm very lucky to have such a loving, supportive, and understanding wife, and I love her "tons and tons."

Index

Ordering additional copies of

FIVE MYTHS
OF CONSUMER
BEHAVIOR

Fax this form to: (206) 269-0444
Or go online to: www.5myths.com
Or call: (206) 529-4184 and have your credit card ready
Or e-mail: orders@5myths.com
Or mail this form to:

ConsumerEase Publishing, PO Box 9906, Seattle, WA 98109-0906

Form #1021

Name: _____

Address:_____

City: _____ State: _____Zip:_____

Telephone: _____ E-mail: _____

Price: $16.95 plus $4.00 shipping (estimated $9.00 international) per book. Washington residents please add 8.8% sales tax.

Number of copies:_____ Total price: _____

Payment:
☐ Check enclosed or ☐ VISA ☐ MasterCard ☐ AMEX

Card number:_____ ___

Name on card: _____ Exp. date:_____